Simply Sasquatch:

A Story More Legendary Than Bigfoot – Your Own!

By Ben Glenn

First publishing 2008
Glenn, Ben
Simply Sasquatch: A story more legendary
than Bigfoot – your own!
Ben Glenn p. cm.

ISBN 978-0-9675680-4-1 (paperback)

I.   *Glenn, Ben*   II.   *Title*

Library of Congress Catalog Card Number: 2008930636

Attention Church Groups:

Quantity discounts are available on bulk purchases of this book for reselling, educational purposes, subscription incentives, gifts, or fund raising. For information please contact Chalkguy Media International at www.chalkguy.com.

Other books by the Author

Big Enough: Finding Faith to Move Mountains
Simply Special: Learning to Love your ADHD

How to Contact the Author

Professional speaker Ben Glenn has been entertaining and educating audiences for more than a decade. He speaks about ADHD, having a positive attitude, achieving personal excellence and spiritual issues to groups all over the world. To discuss hiring him for your next conference, annual meeting, fund raiser or special event, contact:

Polina Osherov
Chalkguy Media International
www.chalkguy.com or 800-763-2609
email: polina@chalkguy.com

Dedication

To Mrs. Kathy Kazmar, who was
obedient and generous.
That $285 has gone
a reeeeaaaly long way!

Acknowledgements

This book is so much better than it could have been thanks to the following patient and hard-working folks:

Polina Osherov
Jocelyn Godfrey
Larry Medcalfe
Phil Studdard
Vladimir Osherov
Randy Hosilyk

Interview with Bigfoot

Q: How long has your kind been around?

A: Sasquatch have been around for hundreds of years. Before Sasquatch arrived here on earth, we were a part of the rebel forces that fought the evil empire. Sasquatch are actually known as Wookies to the rest of the galaxy.

Fact: *Nobody knows how long Sasquatch has been around; sightings, however go back hundreds of years.*

Chapter 1

Some time ago, while I was watching a documentary on The History Channel called Monster Quest (which explores the fact, fiction, and fascination behind legendary monster sightings worldwide) - I birthed an idea. The show that day was about Bigfoot, who also goes by the more fancy name, Sasquatch. Thank God I had my Magic Notebook nearby to take note of my mental creation, or this book would never have existed! On a fresh page, I wrote down the words that popped into my head: "Simply Sasquatch." At first, this was just a funny-sounding phrase that I thought I could maybe use as a comedy bit. Over time, however, the idea actually formed an interesting shape of its own.

The documentary explained how the Bigfoot legend has been around for years, and how most people, young or old, have heard his story. I'm not a scientist or anything, but I decided to do my own experiment to see if this statement was true. So at my next several events, I asked people young and old, "Have you ever heard of Bigfoot?" And sure enough, every single one of them had.

This was amazing to me, and still is... So many people know about a creature whose only proof of existence is some large footprints, a few fuzzy home videos and numerous, unsubstantiated, eye-witness reports.

While the idea for "Simply Sasquatch" percolated in my mind, I continued researching Bigfoot. I rented movies, looked at children's books, Googled "Bigfoot" and

"Sasquatch" (did you know that there is a Texas Bigfoot Conservancy organization?), and even joined a MySpace Club dedicated to sightings of Bigfoot! Yep. I went all out! I learned more about Bigfoot than I ever cared to know.

Why was I so obsessed with the Sasquatch? My wife proposed that my infatuation with the elusive creature was a long-lost family connection. When I looked at her quizzically, she pointed out that the family resemblance was quite striking; the Sasquatch was really hairy and so was I. The Sasquatch left big footprints, and I had pretty large feet myself. She listed a few other potential similarities that I won't bore you with, but let's just say that after that conversation, she found herself sleeping on the couch, one eye open, in fear of her life.

Seriously though, why was I so taken by Bigfoot? The more I thought about it, the more it became clear to me that I am a sucker for a great story. But then who isn't?

✳ ✳ ✳ ✳ ✳ ✳ ✳ ✳

A few years ago, I was invited to speak at the headquarters of Tahitian Noni International in Utah, a company which sells health-related products derived from the tropical noni plant. While I was preparing for the presentation, I researched the company a little more, and was struck by how quickly it had grown and how successful it had become. From 1996, when TNI was founded, to 2000, sales totaled more than $1 billion!! That's a pretty big number! According to www.noni.com, it took Microsoft almost 10 years to make the same amount in sales as it took TNI five! How did they do it, I wondered. A good friend of mine, Tracy, a distributor with TNI, explained to me that

TNI had a simple but clearly quite brilliant marketing philosophy – Tell the Story. Instead of doing hard-core sales and high-pressure product pitches, TNI encouraged distributors to simply share the difference that drinking the noni juice was making to their overall well-being and health with anyone who would listen – friends, family, co-workers, people in line at the supermarket. And it worked! Most of us care about our health, and when presented with an opportunity to improve it AND make some money doing so, very few would pass that up. And so TNI exploded and continues to grow globally as new Noni converts continue telling others their story.

Do you see the parallel between Bigfoot, and the TNI? It's all about the power of the story... Everyone knows that stories and story-telling have been around since the ancient times. We humans have shared stories through words, images and sounds in every culture and in every land, serving many functions, ranging from educational to entertaining. Stories never get old – witness the millions of books and movies that exist, and it's clear that people all over the world love a good story. Some stories even have the power to change lives and the course of history. Never underestimate the impact of a powerful account on the lives of people that hear it!

Do you know what is the most influential and powerful story ever told? It has lived on for centuries and has been shared in every language and in every corner of this world. It has changed lives, and altered history. It is the story of Jesus Christ and how He fulfilled His Father's plan to save mankind from a life without hope and salvation. It is a well-documented fact that the Bible is the best-selling book of all time, with an estimated 4 to 6 billion copies distributed worldwide. And the Mel Gibson movie, "The Passion of The Christ," based on biblical accounts of the arrest, crucifixion, burial, and resurrection of Jesus, is North America's largest-grossing R-rated movie of all time, rating 37th worldwide.

Besides the factual stuff, the story of Christ is, I believe, the greatest story of all time. Why? Because it offers the most substantial reward... It may not make you money like talking about the health effects of noni juice might (well, with a few notable exceptions), but the benefit will far outstrip any product that has ever hit the shelves! Can anything beat eternal life?

The amazing thing about the story of Christ is that not only does the story of His life hold amazing power, but when people have a life-changing encounter with Him, the "greatest story" becomes theirs, and not just to live, but also to tell. The beauty of it is that even though all believers talk about the same Jesus, each story is as unique as its teller and each has incredible value.

I think I can already hear you protesting... Don't think you have a story worth telling?

You might be surprised to learn that for a while, I didn't think that I did either, and this was AFTER I started in the ministry and began to travel and speak to different groups. Shocking, but true!

If you are like a lot of folks I know, and struggle with knowing how and why to tell your story, you are going to love this book! By the time you're done reading, you will have discovered the value in your story and will be raring to go and share it with anyone who will listen.

Jesus says in the book of Matthew, "Therefore go, and tell people everything I have taught you."

In essence, He is telling us to go and share the story of our walk with Him. And it's not just about spreading the Good News. I happen to believe that telling our story not only blesses those around us, but it actually blesses us more. In fact, our spiritual health depends on it!

To get you in the story-telling mood, I'm going to share a couple of stories with you. One is a story my ADD brain came up with based on the biblical encounters that Jesus had with lepers. (So don't hold it against me if there is some stuff in there that is not totally factual, because I let my imagination go... But the meat and meaning of the story is what I want I really want to get across). The other is a story that you're probably familiar with if you've ever heard me speak in the Christian setting – it is my story of how I met Christ. I hope you enjoy both and that they get you thinking about your own story. That is the purpose of this book: to help you uncover and reveal your story.

cartoon copyrighted by Mark Parisi, printed with permission

Chapter 2

A horse-drawn cart rounded the corner of the dusty road, moving at a stately pace guided by two large, brown-grey horses, dutifully pulling their solid, rectangular burden. A man sat on the front bench, holding the reins loosely in his worn hands with an ease born of years of experience. The woman sat next to him, her head covered in a colorful scarf, as she half-turned to the back bench, listening to her two young boys talking excitedly, their voices carrying in the still, noon heat.

"Do you think he will tell us the story again?" said the younger boy, his eyes gleaming with excitement as he kicked and swung his legs, his feet not quite touching the floor of the carriage.

"I'm not sure, Dear," responded the woman, smiling at her son with a mixture of pride and exasperation. "Great Grandpa is getting quite old so you boys need to take it easy on him today. I don't want him all worn out and ready for bed before we cut his birthday cake. We want to celebrate his many years to the fullest, and that's not going to happen if he collapses from tiredness before the sun even goes down."

"Aww, Mom! He's going to be fine! Eighty is not THAT old! Look at Abraham from the Bible; didn't he live to be like 150? … No, 170…Wait! One-hundred and seventy-nine years old!?" the boy exclaimed proud of such a creative argument.

"Abraham lived to be 150-years-old, Sammy," the older

boy corrected dutifully as he rolled his eyes.

"Well, whatever, it was it's still heaps older than Great Grandpa!" Sammy fired off passionately in his brother's direction, a little annoyed, but undaunted.

On the front bench, Rachel sensed the tensions growing between her two boys. The ride had already been long for them, and no doubt the boys were growing both weary and hungry. Thankfully, her sons generally got along quite well. They were only two years apart in age, and that meant when things between them were good, they were great, but when they started to get on each other's nerves, all bets were off. Today, with excitement and expectations running high, her sons were already hinting that they would be a handful.

"Stop touching me! MOM!! Tell Sammy to stay on his side of the wagon!" Nathan yelled in frustration as he attempted to shove his little brother as far from him as possible.

Meanwhile, Sammy had dug in with no intention of budging, his left foot firmly planted onto the side of the wagon, his hands gripping the bench. "You're the one's who's touching me, and I AM on my side of the wagon. My side is just bigger than your side, so there!" Sammy squeezed out through clenched teeth, fully focused on winning this particular power struggle.

The man had had enough. "If you boys don't stop this nonsense right this minute, I will turn this cart around and we can all just go home," he said over his shoulder to the two red-faced, sweaty kids in the back. "We can just skip your Great Grandpa's big day. It's YOUR choice! So what's it going to be?"

"He started it," Sammy muttered under his breath in

hopes to get in the last word.

"What? Did someone just say something back there?" Eli said, slowly turning to look at the boys, a menacing frown on his face.

Shaking their heads "no," the boys quickly rearranged themselves, each sliding as far from the other as he could. They knew when their father meant business, and now was definitely no time for a petty squabble. There was no way that they would ever voluntarily skip the best birthday party in the world.

"I'm so glad that we understand each other," Eli commented as he turned his eyes back on the road, rolling his shoulders and stretching his neck. He was hot and tired and the kids had been peppering Rachel and him with questions all morning, chattering up a storm, laughing and singing. He smiled ruefully remembering those days of long ago when he had all kinds of energy. He sighed, hoping that Rachel wouldn't notice, but of course Rachel never missed a thing and she knew exactly what he was thinking.

"Boys, we still have a good hour to go. Why don't the two of you get a quick nap? Today is a big day and it will be a late night too, so rest is just what the doctor ordered," Rachel said, smiling at her sons, reaching out and messing with Sammy's hair.

"Mom, you always say that when we go to Great Grandpa's house. You know what I think? I think you're just trying to get us to be quiet," Nathan said with a small pout, determined not to take a nap. "Besides, I'm too old for naps anyway," he concluded, crossing his arms over his chest and staring off into the distance defiantly.

Rachel laughed a little. "And what's wrong with a little

peace and quiet?" she asked, smiling at her two boys. "All the same, I'm not trying to trick you," she said. "I really do want you two to be ready for tonight and to enjoy yourselves. And this being the day you both look forward to the most throughout the year, don't you want to be fresh for all the festivities?" She sensed that she was not getting through to Nathan and she needed him on board with this in order to convince Sammy of it as well. It was time to try a different approach. "All your cousins are going to be there today," she said, looking at her oldest innocently, "I heard, Nathan, that they are planning on having another dodge ball tournament this year."

Sammy smirked as he recalled the events of last year's big game. Noticing his expression, Nathan scowled and became very interested in his shoes, staring down at them intently. Rachel could see that she finally had Nathan's full attention. "You know, Nathan, I think the reason your brother did so well last year is because he slept the whole way to Great Grandpa's house. Isn't that right, Eli?"

Eli, half asleep and not paying attention, didn't really know what Rachel was talking about, but after 10 years of marriage, he was trained. "Yes dear; that sounds about right," he answered, not skipping a beat.

"So this year, instead of striking out the first round, maybe you could take a nap now and have the energy to stay in the game longer. What do you think?" Rachel felt badly for reminding her son of such a humbling moment, but she knew that she had a good point; plus Eli and she really could use a few moments of quiet.

After a long pause, Nathan grabbed his blanket and pillow and climbed into the back of the wagon without a word. Sammy watched him trying to find a comfortable spot on the hard wood of the wagon. Rachel was hoping that Sammy would follow Nathan; however, he had something on his mind.

"Mom, are you mad?" he asked, looking at her, the corners of his mouth turned down and quivering slightly.

"No Sammy, of course not! Why would you say that?"

"Do you want to get rid of Nathan and me?" He looked at her, his brown eyes big and threatening to fill with tears on a moment's notice.

"Don't be ridiculous, Sammy!" Rachel exclaimed, swinging around all the way to face him. "I love you boys. I would never ever want to be rid of you!"

Sammy refused to be convinced. "Do you still love Nathan and me?" He looked so sad and defenseless sitting there, looking at her with this huge question hanging between them.

Rachel almost started crying, but instead she moved to sit next to Sammy, putting her arms around the more sensitive of her two sons. She squeezed him until she knew there was no debate about her love. She kissed him and said, "Sammy, I love both Nathan and you very much and because I do love you, I want what's best for my two boys. So what I need you to do is to take a nap right there next to Nathan. Please trust me that this is the best thing for you right now, okay?"

"But Mom! I'm way too excited to sleep," Sammy declared, heartened by her hug and kiss. "I'm bigger and stronger than last year. I really don't think I need a nap!"

"I have an idea," Rachel said, pooling all her creative

resources to convince her youngest to take a nap. "Why not, instead of counting sheep to fall asleep, you close your eyes and try to remember your favorite stories that Great Grandpa has ever told you?"

"You mean like the dark and spooky cave, or the guy in the chains, or the pigs…?"

Rachel gave Sammy another little squeeze before he got too carried away. She looked into his eyes so he knew she meant business, and in a calm, deep, hypnotic voice said, "Find a spot in the back, close your eyes and take a nap."

Sammy instinctively looked over at his father to see if he could get him to intervene, but Eli was engrossed with watching the road and trying to stay awake, and would be of no help.

Sighing, Sammy slid off the bench, and curled up with his favorite blanket. Less than a minute later, he was out cold, just like his older brother.

After surveying her sleeping sons for a few more moments just to be sure that they were sound asleep, Rachel returned to her post by Eli's side. They exchanged a glance that spoke a sentiment that no two tired parents ever needed to say out loud: "Finally! Peace and quiet!"

Interview with Bigfoot

Q: How tall can a Sasquatch get?

A: Well, when I am having a good hair day and I stand up straight, I am almost 8 feet tall. Most days, however I am only 7 feet and 2 inches tall, and that's because I have back problems from having to walk all hunched over and everything.

Fact: *Most Sasquatch sightings have reported that the creature was between 7 and 8 feet tall.*

Chapter 3

Up until the third grade, I was much like any other young boy. I loved Legos and army guys; I was convinced that all girls had cooties and should be beamed to Mars; and I believed that the best part of a school day was lunch and recess. Like all young kids, I was much more into playing around than getting a good education. I was carefree, and other than the occasional grounding for typical adventure-seeking boy behavior, I was a happy kid.

Then one day, everything changed. And it all started with a test.

The school discovered that I was struggling in all kinds of ways. They wanted to know exactly why I struggled so they could help me.

Several days of testing landed me in a special education class with some strange and life-changing labels. The tests revealed that I had Dyslexia and as a result was Learning Disabled. Later on I would also discover that I had Attention Deficit Disorder (my biggest challenge), though at the time of my tests, ADHD was not as well recognized and tests for it were not wide-spread as they are now, but it was definitely there. All they knew was that I didn't learn like other kids and that it was a bad thing. The labels were supposed to help explain my difficulties in the classroom, but all they did was make me feel like a freak.

As I look back to that time, I realize that the school had

only good intentions in labeling me and placing me in a special classroom. Like most children, however, I didn't see the upside of my circumstances at the time. I just felt like a stupid kid who had been singled out in the crowd.

Today, statistics indicate that as many as 1 out of every 5 people in the U.S. has a learning disability of some kind (23rd Annual Report to Congress, U.S. Dept. of Education, 2001) and that there are as many as 15 million people (kids and adults) out there with A.D.D! (The American Journal of Psychiatry, June 2007) In spite of these numbers, most people seem to know only a little bit of what it means to have an LD or ADHD. And that "little bit" is mostly negative.

After my years of research and taking classes, I have concluded that there are ironically some great blessings in being an ADDer and being "neurodiverse" (a word that means that there are many different types of "smarts" and that one is not necessarily better than another). In fact, in 2007 I published a book stating that I have come to a point in my life where I can actually claim, "I love having A.D.D." My work is, in fact, largely motivated by the hope that others who are facing the same struggles that I do, will one day adopt the same conclusion.

Before I came to this bold conclusion about my disorders, however, my view on the matter was much the opposite. I did not see my A.D.D. as a gift. It's tragic but true: when a school places a label like A.D.D. or L.D. on a child, he or she cannot help but hear that inner voice asking questions like, "Am I stupid? Am I a mistake? What's wrong with me?"

While I was in elementary school, I battled with these questions daily. I watched all of my friends attend normal classes while I headed off to the small prison-like special ed classroom.

When I entered middle school, my disorders were accompanied by teasing, name-calling, and fights. As all of my efforts to find my way in middle school failed, I gave in to anger. I was mad at everyone and everything. Hatred and pain consumed me. I hated everyone, because in my eyes, everyone around me was normal and I was the singled-out, dumb, special-ed retard. I dreaded each day I had to go to school. I would walk into the building feeling like God had taken all the leftovers from making everyone else, and slapped them all together and called the resulting mess, "Ben Glenn." I felt like an open-box item on the clearance shelf at Wal-Mart: missing pieces, on sale for two easy payments. "Oh, forget the payments! If anyone's willing to take this junk, they can have it for free! Okay, tell you what. We'll pay you to take it." That's how devalued I felt.

I developed a rage issue, not born out of my actual circumstances, but out of the lack of hope I felt for my life. In high school, the name-calling gave way to simply being left out. No clique wanted me. No one thought to invite me to a birthday party. It was like I didn't really exist. I wasn't sure what was worse: to be ridiculed, or to be invisible. I now know that surviving high school outside of a clique is not life threatening. At the time though, I felt like I wasn't going to make it, or shouldn't bother wanting to do anything because I was just a nobody.

What was far more sad though was that when other students got bored with calling me names, I made up for it by doing it to myself, becoming a pro at bullying myself. I called myself some of the most horrific names you can imagine. It is true; no one beats you up better than you beat up yourself.

The upside of my anger and rage was that it made me into a beast of a football player. It was hard though to contain the anger to the field. The day I had my younger brother's head in my arms, ready to snap his neck over him stealing a pair of my socks, was the day I started thinking about the road I was heading down. Since I was so afraid of what I could do in my rage, I built an emotional brick wall around my heart and began to internalize the pain I felt. I continued to hate, but instead of letting it out, I kept it all inside, focusing it on myself. After weeks and months, these walls grew thick and did their job; they kept everyone out and me alone.

In the ninth grade, I looked no different than other boys my age-- just a kid trying to make it through high school. In fact, ninth grade started better than any other school year because I had a great new special ed teacher, Mrs. T. I also had grown several inches over the summer, made the basketball team, and was playing for a great coach. The problem was that by then, I had already dug a hole and fallen into it. On the outside, everything looked okay, but on the inside, I was a total mess.

It was a long road to get from then to now, but to speed the story up for a moment so that you get to the good part, the pain I felt in ninth grade was good for something. Today, I am blessed to speak in many schools across the country. When I walk down the hallways of these schools, I notice the students and am overwhelmed by the idea of how many of them are broken on the inside, but nobody knows it because, like me, they have internalized all the hurt, pain, and junk. I feel lucky, in a strange way, that I can relate to these kids because I've been there.

In the ninth grade, however, I was on the path to just one place: self-destruction.

BIGFOOT AND HIS DOG.

Chapter 4

The wagon continued to ramble along the well-traveled road as the boys slept. Rachel and Eli enjoyed the relative quiet of the morning, each lost in personal thoughts. Now that Rachel could actually hear herself think, she couldn't help but remember how much she used to look forward to her grandfather's birthday celebrations when she was a little girl. It seemed like people from all over would come out to celebrate his birthday with him. She never questioned his popularity – after all, he was one of her favorite people in the world! It did not surprise her that others loved him as much as she did.

Back in those days, her whole family lived close to one another. Everyone took it for granted that they would always be together, but hard times and a need for work sent them to different corners of the country. Rachel sighed as she thought back to the day her parents had packed the wagon and moved her two sisters, two brothers, and her to a place where her father could find work. Her parents had begged Grandfather to come with them, but he would not leave Jerusalem. He would not leave the place where it all happened, and who could argue with that? And so a tradition started. Every year on his birthday, the whole family would come together for a grand celebration.

Rachel looked over at her husband and was filled with joy at having married such an understanding man. Every year without hesitation, he had been willing to participate in this family tradition. She knew that the brunt of the work fell on his shoulders in having to pack and travel such a great distance, and yet he never complained. In fact, during the past few years, she sensed that his participation in this event was more than mere duty. He too was excited to make the trip and spend time with her family. And it wasn't just about the food, drinks, games, and music. It was also about the story. The Story.

Eli nudged Rachel, gently bringing her out of her reverie. "What's on your mind, my love?" he asked quietly so as not to wake the boys.

She smiled at him, "I am so excited to see everyone. Thank you for doing this," Rachel said, putting her arms around her husband and giving him a kiss.

"Now that's what I'm talking about," Eli growled jokingly.

Their tender moment was suddenly shattered.

"I SEE it! I SEE it!" Sammy's jubilant screams filled the air.

Rachel jumped and Eli gritted his teeth.

"Sammy, you do not need to scream," Rachel said without turning around.

"Nathan! I SEE IT! Sammy continued yelling as he shook his older brother awake, not wanting him to miss the best part about getting to Great Grandpa's house.

"WOW! It's really gotten a lot bigger; hasn't it Sammy?" Nathan said in amazement, pointing at the cypress towering well above all the other trees.

Before either Rachel or Eli could open their mouths to protest, their children were already in the midst of launching themselves over the side of the wagon. Out of all the traditions that came with this annual trip, wagon diving was Rachel's least favorite. It was dangerous and unnecessary, she thought.

Eli had come up with this gem a few years back. The side road to Great Grandpa's farm was long and windy. One year, Eli and the boys discovered that cutting across the field and through the woods instead of following the turns of the road was much faster; thus wagon diving was born.

Just then, as the wagon crossed the bridge over Elam Creek, Eli slowed down just a bit and yelled, "NOW!"

Rachel looked away for a second, afraid of the outcome of her boys leaping off the moving wagon; she heard screaming and turned quickly expecting the worst. To her relief, however, the boys were just rolling around in the field, their joyful laughter and yelling carrying into the distance.

"You know how much I hate this!" Rachel said punching Eli in the arm.

Eli winced slightly, then grinned at her, "Yeah, but it sure looks fun; doesn't it?"

Interview with Bigfoot

Q: I know this is a little bit personal, but what do most Bigfoot weigh?

A: Last time I hit a scale, I was pushing about 700 pounds. Now before you go all Jenny Craig on me, that's normal for a Bigfoot; most of those pounds are hair anyway. My cousin, Freddy the Yeti, who's topped the scales at 800 pounds, lost a bet and had to shave his whole body. He weighs 185 pounds now.

Fact: *Predictions have been made that a Sasquatch could weigh anywhere from 650 to 800 pounds.*

Chapter 5

God's timing is something that has always amazed me. He is never early and He is never late. God is always on time. He moves at exactly the right moment.

One of my favorite accounts in the Bible shows God's timeliness when Lazarus, one of Jesus' friends, dies. This story is a must-read with a killer twist at the end. I am going to give you my quick version of the story but you should read it for yourself, in the Book of John, Chapter 11.

Jesus got word that his friend was sick and that he should hurry to his aid. But instead of rushing, Jesus took his sweet time. Meanwhile, Lazarus died and was buried in a stone tomb. When Jesus finally arrived, Lazarus had been dead and buried for four days. Jesus had an encounter with Martha, one of Lazarus' sister, who was quite annoyed that Jesus dilly-dallied, saying to him accusingly, "If you had been here, my brother would not have died."

And what did Jesus do? Well, he didn't even bat an eyelash, and that's because he knew how the story would end. And the way it would end would blow everybody out of the water: Jesus raised Lazarus from the dead. Can you imagine that?

Without knowing this would be the outcome, it's not hard to see how Mary, Martha, and most likely Lazarus would have preferred that Jesus had come and simply healed Lazarus without having to go through the whole death part. But it all came down to trust.

And it still does, doesn't it? We must learn to trust Jesus, even when what God is doing in our lives makes no sense to us at all.

Jesus' timing held many lessons for everyone involved. Why did Jesus delay? What was the purpose behind his "late" arrival? I think that Jesus wanted to use the situation as a visual parable. He wanted to show everyone how much God was capable of doing even in the worst situations. In this instance, those around him learned that Jesus could reach out and save them even when all hope was lost, that he was even bigger than death itself. Back in Jesus' day, maybe everyone was getting jaded about his miracles of healing. Maybe he wanted to shake everyone up and remind them of the awesome power of the Almighty God. The Lazarus story did the trick!

This story is still powerful today, reminding us that God can do anything, even at the eleventh hour, to save us from destruction. It is a parable reminding us to trust God's timing, and God's power.

So back to my story, one thing I have learned about God's timing is that it hardly ever coincides with mine. If I were the only author of my story, I would have written it totally differently. My timing would have rescued me from all my struggles a day or maybe a week after I was first diagnosed.

Instead, in His wisdom, God allowed me to try and make my own way. I believe that He wanted me to learn first-hand that on my own, I was not going to get very far.

Seven years after my initial diagnosis, I hit emotional and spiritual rock-bottom. All hope was gone. I was really ready to be rescued. And that's when God showed up, though I dare say that He was there a lot sooner; I was just not ready to listen to Him. And so the time was right and God intervened and He decided that He would do it through a teacher and a coach named Kathy Kazmar.

Ninth grade went by quickly for me. I had had a pretty good year battling with my learning disabilities. I had a great special-ed teacher and a wonderful basketball coach who helped me every step of the way.

Despite the vast improvement from the hellish years I spent in middle school, however, I still hung onto the defense mechanisms I adapted from all the name calling, teasing and joking other kids did at my expense. I hung on to the anger believing that it was the one thing protecting me from all those who wanted to hurt me. I had my walls and I was still hiding behind them.

Mrs. Kaz, as everyone called her, was a teacher I had very little interaction with in the ninth grade. I saw her around the lunchroom and maybe a few times during gym class. All I really knew about her is that she was well-liked at Plainfield High School. Since I didn't attend any of her classes, I had very little opportunity to get to know her other than what I observed in her interaction with other students. But in those situations, I found her to be a very kind and approachable person.

By the end of the year, Mrs. Kaz had become just another teacher in the lunchroom. I didn't think much about her presence, other than that she was the symbol of authority that kept kids from hurling their shakes across the room.

Like most kids, lunchtime was my most cherished hour during the school day, and it wasn't because the food was all that good; rather lunch was a break from the educational grind of classes. Somewhere, some overachiever said that replacing recess with more classroom time as kids got older would increase productivity, or make the kids smarter. I'm here to officially pronounce that whoever came up with this is CRAZY, especially when it comes to kids with A.D.D! With lunch being my only break, it became a sacred and a much needed time for me to process and decompress.

I don't think the cafeteria at Plainfield High School was any different than those you would find in most other high schools. It was a big room with long tables that smelled like stale milk and bad pizza. After the first few weeks of school, cliques formed and different areas of the cafeteria became "home" to different groups of kids. The popular kids made their choice first, then everyone else filled in around them.

I too had my special spot where I ate every day. But unlike most kids, I liked to eat by myself, something I learned to do in middle school after a practical joke at my expense that involved chocolate pudding and my white Don Johnson pants. What can I tell you? Walking around with chocolate stains on your backside all day leaves a lasting impression.

Well it wasn't pudding, but another incident caused me to finally come to know Mrs. Kaz one on one. It was about a month before school let out for summer vacation. You could tell vacation was getting close as everyone was getting a bit antsy and the lunchroom was full of students who had the kind of energy that could only be alleviated by a three-month vacation. I found my usual spot and concentrated on eating my food, though it was a bit hard not to be distracted by a food fight that was about to get started a few tables down from me. Teachers moved in quickly to intervene, but not before a single milkshake was slung across the room, and hit about three feet from my table, spraying my pants with white frothy goodness. Good thing I wasn't wearing my favorite pair of parachute pants.

The culprits were apprehended and escorted to where they would receive a speedy trial, and the cafeteria resumed its normal comings and goings. I sighed, wiping the milkshake spray residue off my legs, and that's when Mrs. Kaz sat down next to me. I thought maybe she wanted to take my statement to ensure the conviction of the cafeteria bandits, but I was wrong.

Mrs. Kaz put her hand on my shoulder, looked me in the eyes, and said, "Ben I've been praying for you."

This caught me completely off guard. At first I didn't know what to say. No one had ever told me that they were praying for me. It felt a little nice to know at first, but then I got suspicious and my walls went up.

I thought about it for about a second and then the words tumbled out, "Why don't you go pray for someone else and leave me alone."

The thing about walls is that they serve one purpose, and that's to keep things out. It does not matter whether something is good or bad; when the walls are up, nothing can get through.

Mrs. Kaz had something good to bring in my life, but my walls were fortified, and so my response to her telling me of her prayers was a simple, raw, uncensored rudeness. I thought for sure that she would get up and leave my table in tears. Instead, she just smiled at me, as though she wasn't surprised to hear my response. Then she started telling me why she was praying for me and what she hoped her prayers would accomplish. I don't recall a whole lot from the encounter other than the fact that she wasn't going to leave me be. I was taken aback by her boldness. I thought my defenses had been impenetrable and my technique of appearing not to care finely-tuned. I had no idea what to do with her. She had just taken me some place I had never been before.

All of a sudden, Mrs. Kazmar said, "Ben, would you want to go to a summer camp in July?"

I had never been to a summer camp. My only notion of what camp might be like came from watching the movie, "Meatballs," and that had the potential to be fun.

"Are there going to be any girls there?" I asked.

"Yes," she said with a smile.

I didn't hesitate. "I'll GO!"

She gave me a registration form to fill out. I looked at it and quickly noticed that it would cost $285. The wind vanished from my sails. I knew that there was no way my dad would agree to spend that kind of money on a week of me having fun. Our family was already on such a tight budget.

As if sensing my concern, Mrs. Kazmar pulled out a checkbook, "We are able to scholarship a few students to come to camp each summer. I know God has a plan for your life and I would hate for you not to be able to go because of money. So…"

She wrote a check for the full amount for the cost of the camp and told me to bring back the completed registration form as soon as possible. Then she patted me on the shoulder, smiled and left.

I finished my lunch and pondered the encounter. I didn't feel much differently than before except that I was now looking forward to summer more than ever. But inside, a more fundamental shift had begun. There were now small cracks in my walls.

Chapter 6

The sun was setting on yet another fantastic birthday celebration. The day had been filled with laughter, games, delicious food and fellowship. The children and teens were sprawled around the fire pit, stuffed to the gills and weary from a day of running around. Just one boy looked like he still had energy left in his body; it was Nathan. He sat, his back straight, smiling and glowing with pride. This time, he'd been the one left standing after a numerous and sweaty bouts of dodge ball. And no victory had been sweeter than this one. His older cousins had carried him around on their shoulders, addressing him as Sir Nathan, as was the tradition, feeding him grapes and treating him like royalty. This was the best day of his life!

It was almost time for Great Grandpa to tell his story. The adults were bringing out blankets, chairs and stools and joining their children on the clearing around the fire. Huffing and puffing under its weight, Eli carried out a large, wooden armchair and set it down facing the group. Great Grandpa would soon take his seat there. Upon the placement of the chair, the semi-comatose group of kids stirred, summoning enough energy to attempt jostling for the spots closest to the armchair – not one of them wanted to miss a single word that fell from Grand Grandpa's lips.

When almost everyone was seated and the clearing seemed to be completely filled with people, Great

Grandpa Levi came out, his arm linked through Rachel's. The two of them walked slowly through the parting crowd. Conversations and laughter began to die down as everyone got ready to listen to the greatest story they'd ever heard before.

Levi finally took his seat, and cleared his throat, 'Thank you all for being here with me once again," he looked around smiling. "How blessed I am! Never in a million years could I have imagined going from a life of being wrapped in dirty bandages to this," he said spreading his arms to encompass everyone around him.

"Why were you covered in bandages, Great Grandpa?" asked Zachary, one of the younger children, who'd never heard the story in its entirety but only bits and pieces of it from his older siblings.

"He had nasty gross sores everywhere," blurted out Sammy, frustrated with Zachary's interruption. "You need to pay attention, Zach!"

"It's okay, Sammy. If I was Zachary, I'd want to know the answer to that question as quickly as possible too!" said Levi, proudly looking over four generations of his family. Eighty years old...WOW, he thought, I never thought I'd make it this far. He blinked back tears as he looked around at his family settled comfortably on chairs and carpets spread across the ground. Back when he was wrapped in all those bandages, the idea of a family had been as impossible as a cure for his ailment. He stared for a long moment at the attentive crowd without really seeing them. Then all of a sudden, he realized that his silence had passed the dramatic pause stage.

"Are you okay, Grandpa?" Rachel had come up to check on him, concerned. She touched Levi on the shoulder and reflexively he started as though surprised that her hand was there.

"Yes, Rachel, I'm fine. Just an old man trying to gather his thoughts." He smiled and patted her hand. Rachel looked relieved and returned to her seat.

He had been telling his story for the better part of six decades. He was a master storyteller, knowing every way to use his voice, face and hands to create drama.

But some of the years when he told story, he didn't feel like it had been real. Sometimes he felt like he was not talking about himself at all, but somebody else.

Today, however, was different. Today, he could taste the dampness of that cave on his tongue and smell the stench of dirty bandages wrapped around his arms and legs.

"Where did you get all the sores, Great Grandfather?" Zachary asked as he crawled into Levi's lap, finally bringing him out of his reverie. "Did you fall into a prickle bush? One time I fell into a prickle bush, and boy did it ever hurt!" The boy grimaced as he remembered the incident.

Levi had to laugh, "No, Zachary. I didn't fall into a prickle bush, but there was that one time when I ran into a cactus… But that's a whole other story." He smiled at the boy, ruffling his curly, black hair affectionately. "Why don't you have a seat right up front here in this special chair?"

Levi gently set Zachary on a small, red chair padded with a sheepskin, its back decorated with fancy swirls, then got back to his own seat and took a deep breath. He was about to share one of the most amazing stories anyone had heard.

"I was just old enough to start going to the temple when

I first noticed the sores. I didn't know where they came from or why, but I tried to hide them because I worried what people might think. Eventually though, my mother noticed the sores and took me to the temple doctor and that's when everything went downhill for me. I couldn't attend the temple anymore or school. My mother wouldn't let me go outside much and people started talking badly about me, even kids who I thought were my friends." Levi paused and took a deep breath. Even after all these years, the rejection he had experienced stung.

"I also overheard one of our neighboring busybody housewives say that one of my parents or grandparents or great grandparents must have done something really evil and that is why I was sick, that God was angry at our family and that he sent the leprosy as a punishment." Levi paused again, aware suddenly that the large crowd around him was completely still, all eyes on him.

"Leprosy," a word that still struck fear into the heart of anyone who heard it. Yes, he had had leprosy.

Today, years later, as he sat in the chair and recounted his story, he no longer believed that God had sent him leprosy as a punishment; but back when he was a boy, the thought had terrified him. He had looked up at the sky from beneath his brows, afraid to tip his head back all the way in case God decided to punish him again for being disrespectful, and asked in a small voice, "Why God? Why?" All he knew is that his family went to the temple and did everything that the Torah commanded. He'd heard his parents arguing one night about which side of the family had committed the horrible misdeed that had resulted in his sickness. Yet at the end of that conversation, both agreed that they could not think of a single thing that would require so severe a punishment. And so there were no answers. All Levi knew is that one day he was a regular kid playing outside with his friends and the next he was an outcast with a death sentence.

"I had just started thinking that girls were cute," Levi said with a small smile, "And how I wanted to apprentice to my uncle Sam to be a stonemason…"

"That's gross!" Zachary interrupted, unable to hold back his disgust at the notion that any girl could be considered cute. He was immediately hushed by everyone around him and sat back in his chair, disappointed that no one else seemed to share his disapproval.

"Anyway," Levi continued, "It wasn't very long before the neighbors forced my parents to take me to a leper colony and leave me there. That was the worst day of my life."

And it was. Even now, his heart ached with the horror of it. He saw his mother's tear-streaked face in his mind's eye, clear as day. He heard her sobs as his father led her away, leaving Levi standing alone, a sack of clothes and provisions at his feet, a rocky, cave-pockmarked hill behind him. And then he tipped his head up and looked at the sky, shook his fist at it even, and yelled obscenities that he'd heard some of the older kids use. He wanted God to strike him down. He wanted to be dead. It seemed to him that death was the only way that he could stop the pain that was ripping up his insides. All hope was gone. His family had abandoned him; he was sick and alone. What future other than death could be better?

But God did not strike him down. The sky remained silent and unresponsive. Who knows how long he would have stood there if not for an old man who appeared from nowhere, took him by the arm, and led him to a small cave on the far side of the hill.

"You can stay here," he told Levi gently, setting down the small bag that contained everything that Levi now owned. "We eat breakfast at sunrise and you are welcome to join us." With that, he left the boy alone.

It was many days before Levi could go without crying himself to sleep. He didn't know how to feel about his new "family." At first, he was scared of the bizarre looking men and women; but they were kind and gave him food, so it wasn't long before he didn't even see the sores or the bandages. Still, he missed his mom, dad and brothers. Still, he wondered what he had done to earn God's wrath. Months passed. Then years.

"By the time I turned 17, I had resigned myself to my lot in life. I knew that I would be a leper until my dying day. I was angry and bitter. I had hatred in my heart, and God was my enemy." Levi paused for dramatic effect and noticed that Sammy and Nathan sat up in anticipation. They knew that the best part of his story was right around the corner.

"Then one day, just as I was starting to fall asleep, I heard shouts and loud talking coming from the bottom of the hill. I didn't know what was going on, but it looked like everybody was starting to gather down there around a man who was waving his hands and jumping up and down, shouting and laughing. He looked familiar, but I just couldn't figure out where I had seen him before." Levi leaned forward as he relayed this part of the story, looking conspiratorial.

"When I got to the crowd of lepers surrounding the man, I realized in amazement that the man looked familiar because he'd been living in our community all this time. I knew him! It was Simon, a leper just like me. I had not recognized him because his bandages were gone and his arms and legs and face looked smooth and young and disease-free. I was so overwhelmed with trying to understand what was going on that it took me a few seconds to hear what he was shouting as he danced in joy amongst us.

"I'm healed!! I've been made clean! Glory to God! Halleluiah!"

How could this be? A miracle!! Levi remembered experiencing the strangest sensation in the pit of his stomach as he stood there that night, taking in the whole spectacle. The sensation grew and spread from his belly to his chest, gripping his heart with an emotion that he had not known for several long years – hope. And what a wonderful sensation it was. Still, in his bitterness, he did not allow himself the luxury of dwelling on it. Why would God heal him anyway? Hadn't God cursed him with this disease to start with? And so, amidst the laughter and yelling and dancing, he retreated to his cave and put away his foolish thoughts of healing. Maybe God did offer healing, but not to guys like him. He tossed and turned for a long time that night before falling into a restless sleep, filled with strange dreams.

✳ ✳ ✳ ✳ ✳ ✳ ✳

The full moon made it easier to navigate through town in the dark of night. Levi was a master scavenger. He learned early on that many lepers died from starvation and malnourishment rather than from the actual disease.

Being an outcast and feared by people made getting food and good, clean water a challenge. Days had passed since his last decent meal, and he was anxious to get to the town and rummage through the day's garbage.

As he padded softly through the dark streets, he thought about the people asleep in their comfortable beds, and anger started to well up in his chest. These people condemned me to living in a cave. These people have thrown rocks at me. These people call me "unclean" and run from me screaming.

Levi hated them all. His hunger for food had been quickly replaced by a hunger for revenge and violence. He wanted to take all the hatred inside of himself and unleash it on someone.

Now all he needed was an excuse, for someone to give him a reason to lash out. But the streets were quiet and empty except for an occasional stray dog trotting by with a wary look.

Suddenly, he saw it - a light shining brightly at the end of the street as if a door had been propped open. He hurried towards it. He heard voices. It was his chance for payback. He would reveal himself when the time was right and then pity the man or woman to see him and avert his or her eyes first.

Years of sneaking around had him instinctively hug the dark walls as he traveled towards the source of light. Heart pounding in his chest, he inched closer and closer until he could see that two young men were lost in an animated conversation, lit up by the open doorway of a bakery. Travelers Levi concluded. He'd wait until they had finished talking and began heading on their way. He knew they would definitely walk by him, as the street was a dead-end and the only way out was past his hiding spot. They won't see me coming until it's too late. Levi felt the handle of a small axe he always carried in this belt, fingering it nervously.

He'd never done anything like this before. But he was beyond caring. If he was ever caught, what could they possibly do to him that was worse than what had already been done? He thought again of all the injustices and his blood boiled.

What was taking these men so long? It seemed like an eternity had passed since he'd crept up and positioned himself for attack. It was strange really that these two were out in the middle of the night, on the street with not a care in the world. Didn't they realize that danger lurked in the shadows? Rich people! Must be nice to live with not a care in the world. He rolled his shoulders trying to ease the tension in his neck and back from standing still for so long.

Why didn't they start walking already? That must be some conversation they are having! He decided to inch closer to the men as curiosity got the better of him. Bits and pieces of the conversation floated past his ears. None of it made any sense, but he did keep hearing one word that was somehow familiar yet strangely unknown, "Jesus."

Jesus. Jesus? Who was this Jesus? And why were they talking about him?

"...And then he said 'The kingdom of God is near. Repent and believe the good news,'" the shorter man told his friend in an awe-struck voice. "Do you really think that the ancient prophecy is coming to pass even as we stand here talking about it?"

"No question about it, Marcus," responded the other man in a deep voice that Levi found strangely soothing. "Just look at all the miracles that take place wherever He goes, and you can only conclude that Jesus is who He says he is. Truly, God is among us!"

"I have heard the stories, Jonas, but do not know what to believe. It's all people talk about right now, Jesus and his miracles, but ask the temple priests and they wrinkle their noses and act as though the town has gone mad." There was confusion and uncertainty in the man's voice.

"Marcus, I have seen Jesus with my own two eyes drive out an evil spirit, give a blind guy his sight, make countless cripples walk AND though I have not seen this, I have heard it from a reliable source that he healed 10 lepers. Can you imagine that? Who has ever heard of such a thing?"

Levi continued creeping towards the two men, anger forgotten, his attention fully consumed by wanting to hear more about Jesus. Who was this Jesus? He felt like he was supposed to know this person and yet didn't. The urge to hear more was much stronger than he could ever explain. He didn't just want to eavesdrop, he wanted to ask questions, to learn more, but how could he? Surely these men would turn their backs on him, shooing him away as though he were a stray animal. He was having an internal battle unlike anything he'd experienced before.

One voice in his head said, "Go and talk to these men; you need to ask them where you can find this Jesus so that you can know for yourself who he is."

The other voice countered, "No! You're crazy! Hide in the shadows where you belong. Don't you know what will happen if they see you? You crazy fool!"

Who knows how long he would have crouched there waging a war with himself, but a funny thing happened. The axe that had been securely wedged in his belt somehow came loose and clattered to the ground.

"Who's there?" Marcus asked, tentatively straining to see into the shadows that the buildings created. "Jonas, did you hear that? What do you think that was?"

The two men took a couple of tentative steps in Levi's direction. "Probably just a stray cat prowling," Jonas said with a shrug, losing interest.

Offended at being confused with a stray cat, Levi made a decision. He picked up his axe and slowly stepped out of the shadows. "I'm not a stray cat," he said defiantly staring at the two men, his leprosy-covered face naked in the light of the bakery.

The two men turned and stared at Levi and his axe. For a second, no one said anything.

"Can we help you, friend?" asked the man with the deep, soothing voice, gesturing to Marcus to keep still.

Levi wasn't sure what to do. This was not the reaction he was expecting. He cautiously lowered his weapon. "Is it true what you said, about this man, Jesus, healing lepers?"

"Yes," responded Jonas in the same calm voice. "It is."

Levi considered his response carefully. There was no way the men could have known that he was listening to their conversation, so this was no prank. And why would the man lie about this anyway? What would be the purpose? Besides, how is it that he, Levi the leper, was having an actual conversation with one of "them?" He needed more answers.

"Who is this Jesus that you keep speaking of?"

"Jesus is a teacher out of Galilee, and he has been sharing some good news with those of us who follow him. I think he's the Messiah, though many would argue with me," Jonas responded carefully, still unsure if the disfigured man in front of him was planning on hacking him and Marcus into fish bait.

"I can see why you would want to know more about him," he added after Levi didn't say anything in response. "Do you want us to tell you where you can find him?"

All Levi could do was nod. For some reason, he was having a hard time breathing. Something was going on here that was unfamiliar to him. Why were these men speaking with him? Why did they not run screaming? And could Jesus really heal lepers? Oh! If only that were really true!

"You look hungry," Jonas noted. "Can we share some of our food with you?" he asked, not waiting for a response before reaching into his rucksack and pulling out a loaf of bread. He then walked over to Levi, and held the bread out to him. "Here, take it."

Levi numbly reached out and wrapped his fingers around the still-warm bread, its sweet aroma wrapping itself around him, making his stomach growl in protest.

"Thank you," he stammered, suddenly embarrassed to be holding an axe in his other hand. He awkwardly stuck the weapon back in its place.

Just when things couldn't get any stranger, Jonas put his large hand on Levi's shoulder and said, "If you want to see Jesus, keep an eye out for him near the Temple. He goes there frequently to debate with the priests. I'm sure he will be there tomorrow. And for what it's worth, I'm sorry for everything that has happened to you as a result of your condition. I do not know if you will receive healing, but I do know that regardless of what happens in your life, God does love you and has a plan for you." With those words, the man squeezed Levi's shoulder, then turned and walked back to where Marcus was standing.

There was nothing left to say. Gripping the bread with both hands as though his life depended on it, Levi began to hurry down the dark street. He knew that it would soon be awash with the dawn's light and that he needed to take cover. His mind was still reeling from everything that had just taken place, and in his mind, he could not stop repeating it, the name: Jesus. Jesus. Jesus.

Interview with Bigfoot

Q: Being as big as you are, you must have a big appetite. What kind of food do Sasquatch eat?

A: We eat all kinds of things from fruits and berries to fish and meat. We just worked out a real sweet deal with the Keebler Elf people. We promised to stop eating the elves and slowing down their production in exchange for a steady supply of Pecan Sandies.

Fact: *An "average" sized Sasquatch needs approximately 5,000 calories a day to maintain its weight. That's 63 Keebler Pecan Sandies a day!*

Chapter 7

Though my camp tuition was paid for, my father was very skeptical about the idea of me going. The camp was organized by Fellowship of Christian Athletes, and as far as he was concerned, anything with the word "Christian" in it needed to be approached with caution, at best. The recent multiple scandals involving certain tele-evangelists didn't really help. My father was convinced that FCA was nothing more than an elaborate scam to separate him from his money. Thankfully, my father's mom, who was a big supporter of FCA, put in a good word for them and he grudgingly agreed to let me go.

After looking over the camp brochure, I had warmed up to the idea of going to camp. There were basketball courts and football fields and all kinds of activities planned. I wasn't too thrilled about the God stuff that was obviously going to be a part of camp, but I figured I'd play along anyway. Plus, maybe going to camp would finally get God to notice me, and I wanted a chance to air my grievances. I had a lot of complaining stored up!

And, so one humid and hazy July morning, I boarded a bus destined for the FCA National Conference Center in Marshall, Indiana. I had only a vague notion of what to expect when the bus would pull up to camp three hours later. It was a long three hours!

When the bus finally pulled into the camp, I was anxious to get out and explore – the grounds looked beautiful! The camp was nestled on a clearing surrounded by a dense forest. Rustic cabins dotted the hilly landscape. The cafeteria was wisely placed in the middle of the campgrounds, and the smell coming from the building promised that it would be a gluttonous week. The sound of ping pong could be heard coming from the student center as campers were already engaged in competition. Next to the student center was a full basketball court with hoops that held fresh new nets already being assaulted by a group of ambitious players. A gravelly path leading to a small fishing pond snaked its way past a quaint, brown, wood-sided building that I later learned was the chapel. It was a postcard-perfect scene giving me a warm and fuzzy feeling that unfortunately didn't last.

Beautiful surroundings aside, I suddenly began noticing the people whose lives I would be sharing for the next five days. It was obvious that I was surrounded by a bunch of athletes: gym shorts, sneakers and muscled appendages were everywhere. But that wasn't the problem; the problem was that a lot of these kids were wearing white t-shirts which splashed a gigantic white crucifix across their chests. And I saw a lot of Bibles being carried around. Big Bibles. Big Bibles with their own carrying cases. I was starting to get really worried. The final straw was when a group of girls walked by me singing Kumbaya. I started panicking.

My dad was right: I had arrived in the land of freaks! This was a cult I would never be able to escape. Any moment now, someone with brightly colored Kool-Aid would offer me a big sip.

I offered the bus driver 20 bucks to take me back home, but he laughed at me and closed the doors in my face. I watched the bus pull away with the horrible realization that I was now a prisoner of the camp. I checked in at the registration desk, receiving my bedding and room assignment, all the while plotting my escape. "Act normal. Act normal," I kept repeating to myself. I wanted to stay under the radar as much as possible. I figured it was best to wait until nighttime before making a run for it.

Before long, all the buses had left, all the campers had registered and claimed their beds, and it was time for our first meeting as a group. I was herded along with the rest of the group to the chapel.

Inside, the chapel had a wonderful, rustic feel to it. The dark red wood of the walls glowed in the yellow light of the six chandeliers that hung along the chapel ceiling. A huge wooden cross was the chapel's only adornment and it hung high at the front of the building right behind the altar. Suddenly, the song, "Going to the chapel..." took on a whole other visual meaning. This was THE chapel! It was perfect...well, only if you didn't take into consideration all the campers there singing nutty camp songs. One such song, and it was being sung as I was walking into the chapel, was called "Soaring Like Eagles." It is here that I must ask you to try and put yourself in my shoes. I was a kid who had never been to camp, never sung a camp song, hardly ever went to church, and here I was surrounded by 300 students, standing on their chairs, arms outstretched, singing, "I am going to soar like an eagle!"

I thought that if I clicked my shoes together three times while saying the phrase, "There's no place like home! There's no place like home," I could maybe escape this embarrassing nightmare, but I had lent my ruby red slippers to Dorothy. So instead I excused myself and ran to the payphone. I called my mom collect and explained to her that I was being brainwashed into acting like an eagle and that she needed to leave now to come and get me.

If I haven't said it yet, let me say it now: I have a great mom. She is so loving and giving; in fact in the history of all the mothers in the entire world, my mom is one of the best. So I asked my loving mother to come and save her freaked out son from a week of camp, and what did she do? She told me to stay put and to have a good week; then she hung up on me. I didn't think so at the time, but it was the best thing she could have done for me.

After chapel was dinner. I tried to console myself with the idea that while I had to endure a week of total weirdness, at least I would get to eat well. After making my way through the obligatory cafeteria line, out of habit, I stopped and looked for an empty table. There were none to be seen; in fact, almost all the tables were completely filled up with kids. I knew I hesitated too long because I heard someone yell out my name. Confused, I looked at the guy who was calling me, who by the way was the size of house. "Come sit with us," he yelled, waving me over to his table, already half filled with students.

"Do I know you from somewhere?" I asked cautiously certain that I had never seen him before in my life.

"Nope," he answered giving me a big smile

"Well, then, how do you know my name?" I asked more confused than ever.

His smile grew wider, "Ummm, you're wearing a name tag."

I decided to sit down and not do anything further to make a fool of myself. After a quick round of introductions to the five guys sitting around the table, I focused on my food. From past experience, I knew that it would be better for me to say as little as possible and just listen to the conversation. I really didn't want them knowing that this was my first camp experience of any kind because it quickly became apparent that most of these guys were veteran campers. At first, they talked about the sports and games they would get to play during the week. I liked the sound of that, but then, all of a sudden, they got into all the religious mumbo jumbo. They talked about the chapel sessions and their favorite chapel songs. They were all excited to hear the chapel speaker talk about Jesus, and they looked forward to the quiet time they would spend with Jesus while at the camp. I sat there listening, but the more they talked about Jesus, the more curious I got.

I looked at the big kid who invited me to eat with the group, and said," You act like Jesus is coming to camp or something. I've been to church at Christmas and Easter and every time I go I see him stuck to that plus sign. Do you guys really think Jesus is coming to camp this week?"

The conversations paused as every kid's eyes turned on me. Over the years, I had gotten used to getting some strange looks from my classmates for the questions I asked during class, so I steeled myself, preparing for their mockery, nonchalantly taking a bite of a dinner roll and waiting for someone to answer me.

The big kid – Tom - shifted around in his seat as if he were trying to find just the right words.

"That plus sign you mentioned is actually a cross, and that cross means something more than a decoration to hang around your neck."

He paused for a moment and then somewhat abruptly asked, "Ben, do you ever mess up?"

I thought that to be a bit personal, and I was afraid at first to answer thinking I would be giving these few guys sitting around the table ammunition for teasing me later. Feeling like I dropped a tough question on the group, however, I decided to play along but not reveal any specific mess-ups. "Sure I mess up. Who doesn't mess up? We all mess up!"

"You're right. We all do mess up," Tom said as he opened his Bible. "The Bible says 'For all have fallen short.' Which means every one of us has mess-ups in our lives. Ben, let me ask you another question. What happens to you when you mess up?"

I scanned my brain for one of the most benign punishments I had ever gotten. I did not want to give them any real juicy stuff that would expose me for future ridicule. "Well sometimes, when I was real young of course, I had what my mom called a potty mouth, and when my potty mouth would flare up, I would have to chomp down on a bar of soap."

"What would you call that, Ben?"

Was that a trick question? "I would call it 'gross!'" I said making a face. "What would you call it?"

Tom smiled at my response and said, "Well anytime we do something wrong, there is always going to be a consequence. We do something our parents ask us not to do and we get grounded. We say something inappropriate and we have to chomp down on a bar of soap. Consequences. The Bible says, 'For the wages of sin is death.' That basically means that messing up is punishable by death."

At first I didn't believe what he was saying. Was he trying to mess with my head? Was this going to be like the time my friend Phil had taken me snipe hunting? I had never read the Bible; I knew it had been around a really long time and was full of some very interesting stories, but this death stuff I had never heard before. I glanced over to where Tom was pointing in his Bible and saw the words for myself. As plain as day it said we all deserved death. Man, this camp was turning into a real downer. Wasn't there another way? I wanted to ask.

But before I could say anything, Tom continued, "Now before you leave dinner all down and depressed because of this information, let me tell you why we are looking forward to singing songs about Jesus and hanging out with him." He paused and looked at everyone seated around the table. "God loves us so much that he did not want us to die as a result of our mess-ups, so he gave us a gift. He gave us his one and only son. This is where the cross comes into the picture. Jesus, the one you once thought to be nailed to a plus sign, was actually nailed to a cross, and the Bible says it was on that cross Jesus took all the sins of the world upon himself and died as a sacrifice for you and for me, for all of us sitting at this table, all of us sitting in this room."

He paused for a moment, then went on, "That verse about us dying, it ends on a good note, see? For the wages of sin is death, but the gift of God is eternal life in Christ Jesus our Lord. Jesus died for you as a gift to you. The big question is, are you going to accept this gift or not?" With those words, Tom turned his attention away from me as if sensing that I needed time to think and process.

Questions swirled in my mind as the table reclaimed an enthusiastic spirit. The group began talking again about their plans for the week, while I was left to ponder all that I had heard. I thought that God was a joke. I thought he wasn't at all interested in me and my life. I had been to church, but I never really paid much attention. I thought it was just a place people went to in order to make themselves feel better. Not once did I consider that perhaps God loved me. I thought that God was just waiting for me to do something really stupid, so he could zap me like some worthless bug. What did all of this mean?

I had to ask, "Why? Why would Jesus die on a cross for me? I have never met him before. It's not like I go to church all the time. I don't think I even like God. So tell me, why in the world did he send Jesus to die for me?"

Tom rubbed his short-cropped hair, anxious to help me understand. "Ben, the simple answer is that God loves us and wants us to come home to Him in heaven. We do not know why He loves us, but He does. It's kind of hard to wrap your mind around it, isn't it?"

Love.

The tremor I had felt months earlier when Mrs. Kazmar wrote that check was quickly becoming a quake. My walls were under attack and I could feel them giving way. Somehow, at a summer camp in the middle of nowhere Indiana, love began seeping into my fortress.

"Oh, and one more thing," said Tom, looking at me with a big smile. We do expect Jesus to be at this camp. In fact, I know He is here already. I hope this week you have a chance to meet Him. Maybe you can ask Him for yourself why he would do what He did for you when He died on the cross."

cartoon copyrighted by Mark Parisi, printed with permission

Chapter 8

It had been almost two months since his encounter with the two men by the light of the bakery. The following day, Levi did attempt to catch a glimpse of Jesus as He went to the temple to teach, but that turned out to be a bad idea. There was a huge crowd of people, cripples, the blind, yes, even lepers, and all of them were there to see The Teacher. He almost got trampled, catching but a distant glance of the man he most wanted to meet. And so the hope he had received that night slipped away a bit with every passing day, but he still hadn't stopped thinking about the possibility he had heard uttered to him: "God loves you."

It was almost impossible for Levi to believe the words spoken by a strange man. Even before he became a leper, the idea of God's love was something he felt he never deserved. It wasn't that Levi considered himself a bad person, but moreso that he just never saw himself as good enough to be loved.

He had been staring out the entrance of his cave since the sun peeked over the horizon. The bright yellow disk had not even fully detached itself from the horizon, but he could already tell that the day would be wonderful. An urge welled up to go on a long walk, but soon the road to town would be filled with people, animals and wagons and staying put was safer.

Suddenly, a small bird flew into the cave, landing just a few feet in front of him. It cocked its head curiously, looking around for food, then looked right at Levi as if to say, "Why are you just sitting there? Don't you have anything else to do?" Levi almost responded, but caught himself and shook his head, I'm really losing it! Talking to birds now? What next? Snake charming?

He had to go outside for a short break before he lost his mind. Too much time had passed since he had basked in the warmth of the sun. He got to his feet and poked his head out of the cave, squinting as the day's first sun rays hit him square in the face. Everything was quiet. He stepped outside and let the sun play on his skin, warm like a great, big campfire. He took a deep breath and the fresh air burned in his lungs; a joyful reminder that he was outside.

At first he walked along the path that the lepers had worn into the rocky ground. It ran somewhat parallel to the main road, but at some distance from it, a distance that was considered "safe" for travelers on both paths.

Here and there, however, the paths would merge, on bridges and between hills. On such occasions, lepers knew to let all the healthy people pass before first attempting to use the road. Sometimes it would take several hours for there to be an acceptable gap in traffic for a leper to continue on his way. That is why most lepers preferred to travel at night when the road was not so busy. Being alone in the dark sure beat the alternative - hearing loud accusations of "Unclean! Unclean" from passersby, watching people scatter with looks of horror and disgust on their faces, young children crying in fear, old women glaring and cursing.

Levi had almost never traveled the road in daylight and his own sudden recklessness surprised him. Somehow, he had strayed quite a distance from his cave, which was most unusual. It was as if some unseen hand was pulling him along. True, the road was still empty at this early hour, but not for long. Just a bit further, he told himself. I'll walk to the bridge across the Jordan, and then turn back, he made a bargain with himself.

Enjoying the glorious day, he pushed back the fears of humiliation he'd have to face over possibly running into some townspeople before he could turn back. How he hated living with constant fear! Still, today was his day, and he would not let anything ruin it. He walked on, taking in the beauty of his surroundings, breathing deep, a feeling of hope somehow stronger in his heart. As it had done daily for two months, his mind went back to the day when Simon, a leper just like him, had come to see them all fully restored to health. He wished that some day that would be him.

And just like that, he found himself on the banks of the Jordan. He watched the water burble past him energetically. The sun was continuing its steady rise and Levi knew that any moment now, he would hear the gravelly sounds of feet and wagon wheels approaching. It was time for him to turn back. He sighed, angry about having to go back to his cave on such a beautiful day. Alas, he had no choice.

But first, a quick stop by the well – he was really thirsty all of a sudden. Now technically, he was not supposed to be drinking there. If someone caught him, the well would be considered unclean and would require a priest's blessing as well as a special prayer service for it to be declared clean – a huge pain in the neck to say the least.

At that moment, however, he did not care. A priest

taking time out of his busy day to cleanse a well of his despised presence – now there was an inconvenience! He scowled at the unfairness of it. I'm going to drink out of that well and I don't care about what happens. Let the rest of them become unclean alongside of me and see what it feels like. He followed the river south for a few minutes and there was the well, beneath a huge oak tree, protected from the sun by a canopy of gnarled branches and thick foliage.

Levi quickly found a clay pot tied at the neck with thick twine, and lowered it into the dark depths of the well. He leaned on the well's low stone wall, watching the pot disappear and then reappear from the darkness, swinging gently on the rope, sounds of water splashing making him all the more thirsty. He drank hungrily, ice cold water pouring down his chin and neck. He splashed the remainder of the water on his face, trying to remember the last time he had washed his face and feet – it had been weeks. He paused for a moment, listening for any signs of traffic, but all was still. Quickly, he lowered the clay pot into the well one more time, anxious for an opportunity to rinse some of the caked-on dirt from his feet and legs. As he pulled the vessel out of the well for the second time, he caught a brief reflection of his face in the water. He should have just let it go, but he couldn't. He stepped out from underneath the tree and positioned himself so that the sunlight was directly on him. Then, he brought the water jug up to his face and looked again. He almost did not recognize himself. Misshapen and ugly, his sore-covered face looked up at him, further distorted by the ripples his breath made in the water. He was disgusting! No wonder people ran screaming! It took all of his willpower to not smash the water jug against the well. He set it down without using the water. What's the point of being clean when I look like this? He raised his eyes to the blue sky, tears welling up, "God, they tell me that you love me, but look at me. Is this the way you love your children?" There was no response.

Levi began to shake with an uncontrollable fury.

"WHERE ARE YOU?!" he screamed, his fists clenched at this sides. "And why have you done this to me?" All was still. It seemed that even the wind decided to take a break from ruffling the leaves of the big tree above his head. He stood there for a few moments, unsure of what he was waiting for.

And then something inside of him broke. He crumpled to the ground, sobs of despair and futility shaking his body. He'd never felt more alone. God, why don't you help me? How desperate and down do I have to be for you to notice my misery? I just don't understand. My life is crap! Why am I even alive? What possible reason is there for me to wake up every morning? He'd never have given this any thought before today, but he started to think seriously about ending it all. Not like anyone would miss him anyway.

Levi would have probably stayed by the well all morning, plotting his own demise, but God had other plans for him.

Lost in his own thoughts, Levi failed to notice the sounds of the road coming to life. It wasn't until he heard the voices of people approaching the well that he realized that there was no place to hide and he would be forced to declare his presence. Moreover, there was the small matter of his drinking from the well. This could turn quite ugly. He glanced over his shoulder to see a group of men approaching. He knew that he could not count on their sympathy. Looks like I don't need to take matters into my own hands, he thought sarcastically. These men here will probably be quite happy to help me exit the land of the breathing once they realize what I have done. He looked around apprehensively at the large number of rocks littering the area around the tree and beyond. There was little he could do now. He got to his feet slowly and took a deep breath, "UNCLEAN! UNCLEAN! UNCLEAN!" He yelled, his voice cracking on the last "unclean."

Clearly he had taken the men by total surprise. They had been so involved in conversation that they did not notice that anyone was by the well. Now they had come to a stop, their conversation frozen, all eyes on him.

For what seemed an eternity, no one moved and no one said anything. The men and the leper considered each other across the few dozen feet that separated them.

"I think he's been drinking from the well," he heard one of the men say, and the others started grumbling in response.

This was it. Levi sighed, prepared for the worst. In spite of himself, he lifted a silent prayer: God, I'm sorry for being angry and spiteful. I didn't mean it. I guess I just don't understand you, that's all. Please forgive me.

"Oh great! Now what? My goatskin is almost empty and we have a full day of traveling today. I'm going to dehydrate!" A whiny voice came from the back of the crowd.

"Don't worry, Judas. Between us, I think we'll have enough to keep you alive," said a man who stood closest to Levi, his voice steady and calm. He was studying Levi closely, His face unreadable.

"So what should we do?" asked the first man, while the rest of the group looked at the man with the calm voice.

He didn't know why, but Levi knew that somehow, this mystery man held his fate in his hands. He appeared to lead the group, an aura of quiet authority radiating from His face. Besides this calmness, there was something else that Levi couldn't put his finger on.

Without saying anything else, the man began walking towards Levi, closing the gap between them, small puffs of dust punctuating his every step. Levi stood as if rooted to the ground, watching the wind stir up and carry the dust away, afraid to look in the face of the man approaching him. His heart was pounding in his chest. Will He throw the first stone?

"Jesus!" He heard one of the men in the group exclaim. "Where are you going?" Jesus did not respond, and Levi could hear the men starting to talk excitedly, their words making no sense to him as if they suddenly spoke a different language.

Jesus... Where had he heard that name before? Why was it so familiar? Suddenly he remembered, and the realization made him gasp. He felt the hair on the back of his neck and arms stand up, a chill running down his spine. Jesus.

Levi looked up from the ground and found this man standing before him, looking at him with an inexpressible kindness, and something else - what was it - this expression of compassion. It felt as though the man saw to the very core of Levi's being with His clear, steady gaze. The leper suddenly felt a strange warmth spread through his body, as though he had been dipped in warm oil. His limbs tingled with the odd sensation, his head spinning as though he'd been twirling in a circle like he'd done when he was a little boy. The experience seemed to alter time, making everything seem to happen in slow motion.

Jesus stood before him, looking at him expectantly, a small smile touching the corners of his mouth.

Ask him, a small voice inside his head prompted Levi. Go on, ask him!

"Jesus, please make me clean." Levi said quietly, his voice trembling and his body shivering involuntarily. He lifted his gaze and looked Jesus in the eye, hope stirring deep inside of him.

Jesus smiled, placing a hand on Levi's shoulder. "Be clean," He said simply.

Levi closed his eyes, his mind crazed with thoughts, his belly churning from excitement. He felt as though warm oil was being poured on his head, covering every part of his body. More than anything, he felt the hand of Jesus weighing heavily on his shoulder. A solidness like one he'd never experienced in his life embodied that touch. Jesus was more real than real. That made no sense of course, but that's the only way he could think to explain it.

Just then, he knew without a shadow of doubt that the leprosy had left his body. He was clean! He fell, hugging Jesus around the knees, his entire being filled with indescribable joy and relief. "Thank you! Thank you!" he kept repeating, feeling the inadequacy of his words in expressing the overwhelming nature of the gratitude he felt in his soul.

Jesus bent over him, gently prying him away from His

legs, and brought him back to his feet. Levi didn't know what to do with himself. Levi's body was filled with an electric charge making him want to jump, dance and leap, shouting for joy. Now he understood how Simon, the healed leper from his colony, must have felt.

And yet the awe Levi felt simply from being in the presence of this man was even more astounding than being healed... Was it God? Was it divine power that kept Him so mysteriously still and serene? He looked at Jesus and finally knew what it was that radiated from his eyes – love. Yes, love! God did love him! He would never doubt it again. As if reading his mind, Jesus grabbed him and gave him a huge bear hug, and Levi knew that he would never be lonely again.

✳ ✳ ✳ ✳ ✳ ✳ ✳ ✳

Even all these years later, as he told the story to his family, Levi could still feel that hug: more real than real. Tears welled up in his eyes.

"Great Grandfather, why are you crying? Are you hurt?" Zachary asked, offering to get his grandfather a bandage.

Levi thumbed the tear from his eye, unashamed of showing emotions in public. "Come sit in my lap, my boy," he beckoned.

"This may sound a bit odd to you, but my tears are not from pain, but from joy. God was merciful to me that day. Through Jesus, He healed me and brought me back from the brink of darkness. He gave me a new life and a new purpose."

The young boy was nodding but it was obvious that

he didn't quite understand everything that his great grandfather was telling him. Levi decided to try a different approach.

"See, the thing is that when you're a leper, no one is allowed to touch you. Well, no one really wants to touch you anyway. But Jesus, He was not afraid to touch me at all. He showed me what it means to love someone. And He didn't just heal my body, but also my heart. Does that make sense?" Zachary nodded, looking at Levi with big eyes.

"And the other thing is that I really didn't deserve His love and compassion. Just a few moments before I met Jesus, I was shaking my fists at the sky, but Jesus didn't care. He showed me mercy, compassion and love anyway." Zachary was nodding more vigorously.

"I get it! It's like the time when mom took me with her to the city market and told me to stay close, but instead I went to look at the stand with all the toys and got lost. She ended up having half the town looking for me, and when they finally found me, instead of giving me a whipping, she was so excited to see me that she made me my favorite meal and everything. I was worried that she would be really mad, but she was just glad that I was okay." Zachary gave everyone a big grin as chuckles rippled through the crowd at hearing his story.

"You got it, Zachary!" Levi gave the boy an affectionate hug and looked at his audience once more. "Little did I know that day that Jesus came not only to save me, but to save everyone! I followed Him wherever He went until his dying day. And even beyond that...but that's a story for another day," He said with a tired smile.

The story-telling always took a lot out of him, especially these last few years. He wasn't getting any younger, he noted to himself. Soon, he would see Jesus again. The idea made him very excited. He couldn't wait. But for now, he had to share the moral of his story with his family.

"Even though none of you have met the flesh and blood Jesus like I did, you all know the true story of how He changed my life. And because I have told you my story, your lives have been changed by Jesus as well. He lives in your hearts as much as He does in mine and that makes me so happy!"

He smiled as he took in every face looking at him. "And I need you to remember that every single one of you has an incredible story to share with the world about what Jesus has done in your life.

"Some of your stories are still very much in the making," Levi said as he gave Zachary a quick squeeze and looked over at Nathan and Sammy, "But no matter how old you are, the Lord Jesus has touched every single one of you.

"I have been so blessed to share my story with you all these years, but when I am gone, I want this tradition to live on. I want all of you to take turns sharing the story of Jesus, and your story will live on with the generations to come.

"Whenever you are feeling low or things aren't working out the way you planned, think about how God used the life of one young, angry leper to raise a generation of faithful believers, and remember too that this life is but a short interlude before we all get to spend eternity with the Almighty Yahweh!"

Levi liked finishing his story-telling on a high note. And it felt good to be done finally. Plus he knew that they had his favorite dessert waiting for him as a surprise, though it was hardly that after all these years. Still, the dessert was always good, and he loved pretending to be surprised even after all this time.

Q: *I don't mean to be rude, but you really stink. What kind of a smell is that? It's quite robust.*

A: Thank you so much. I do stink and that is something we Sasquatch take great pride in. We actually use our body stench to communicate with one another. You guys have email, but in our world, we have stink mail. If I want to let my cousin Freddy know I am in the area, I just work up a stink and send it down wind. You think I smell now; you should smell me when I have to send a long distance message. Whew! I almost knock myself out!

Fact: *Sasquatch in some areas have been given the name Skunk Ape. The smell of a Sasquatch has been described as rotting flesh, wet hair, creek mud, musky swamp water, and rotten milk. Many believe that Sasquatch have the ability to turn the stench on or off whenever they want.*

Chapter 9

As a parent, I think the payoff for all the sleepless night, the dirty diapers, the projectile vomiting, the teething, and the other hundred things I failed to mention, are the times when your child does something that makes your heart melt. One such moment was last Christmas when she ripped into her gifts, paper shreds flying everywhere, squealing with excitement, and then ran over to give her mom and me hugs and kisses of gratitude. Natty, was enjoying her first "real" Christmas.

"How's that?" you ask, since she is three. Well, when she was just a baby, she had no idea about what was going on around her at Christmas. She just lounged around and drooled a lot, completely ignoring all those colorful packages that had her name on them. She couldn't open her gifts nor was she interested in doing so. Just a baby, doing baby stuff.

I, on the other hand, had a blast opening her gifts for her! (What ADDer doesn't love to rip into shiny, colorful boxes with bows?)

When she was two, Natasha still didn't quite get the idea of presents, and preferred chewing on the wrapping paper and the bows rather than enjoying the contents.

By her third Christmas, however, she had acquired both the skills and the desire to open presents and not just play with the boxes they came in.

Watching her that day made me think back to my first summer camp and the gift that I received there. For the gift of God is eternal life in Christ Jesus our Lord. The first time I really heard those words was when I arrived at camp. What did I have to do in order to get such a wonderful gift? I grew up with my dad telling me that nothing in life is free.

"Even when someone says something is free, it's not really free. There are always strings attached," he would tell my brothers and me.

So if I was going to get the gift of eternal life, would I have to promise to go to church every Sunday? Or would I have to promise to never use cuss words or say mean things about anyone? Perhaps I would have to give half of all I made to the church in order to obtain such a gift? Funny, but not once did it cross my mind that there was nothing on my part that had to been done, that it had already been taken care of.

There is something to be said for leaving everything you know behind, even for a short time, and spending time in unfamiliar surroundings. Taking the time to contemplate your life – where you are now and where you would like to be. Away from your routine, things look much clearer. The camp created an opportunity like that for me.

I had not given God much thought until that week. Much like Levi, the leper, I lived a life of defeat. I didn't have the sores on my body, but I sure had a lot of pain inside. I didn't have very high expectations for my future. I knew I wasn't smart enough to get one of the "good" jobs – there wasn't a doctor or a lawyer waiting to burst out of me. Heck, I could barely read a sentence without stumbling over the words. I could barely write a paragraph without half a dozen errors.

At camp that week, I came to the conclusion that I had become comfortable with the idea of being a mistake. It's hard to believe now, but I was accustomed to people calling me names, and me calling myself names. But worse than that, I was actually kind of okay with it. I guess I didn't know any better. It was a matter of fact that I was the "special" kid and that "special" kids had no great future to look forward to. I'd be flipping burgers in McDonalds, or cleaning tables in a restaurant, or maybe I'd be stuffing sausages at the back of a butcher store for the rest of my life. I had seen other special kids get in trouble, give up and just drop out. I figured that eventually, I, too, would get on the wrong track and end up at a dead end. From a spiritual side, I believed that if God did exist, and if he did have a hand in my creation, then he must not have tried very hard to put me together.

It took years to fully realize and appreciate this: God's love for me is so great that He will do anything and everything to pull me out of my comfort zone in order to open my eyes to the truth. That is what my week of camp was all about, God yanking me out of my comfort zone.

He wasted no time, as that first day I learned that I was pretty much on death row because of my sin. I guess that would be a wake up call for anyone.

Later in the week, I heard a lot about this guy named Jesus and why he died on the cross.

Camp made me really uncomfortable. I didn't know anyone and no one knew me. People were nice and friendly and I didn't know what to do with that. There was singing and Bible studies and talk of heaven and eternal life. An air of kinship grew with each activity and each small group meeting.

It was all too weird. I knew how to deal with hate and indifference and cruelty, but not this. It felt unnatural to be myself and not fear being mocked or put down. It was strange to be included and invited, to belong, and to be... loved?

Not to say that I had never experienced any love; of course I had – from my parents and grandparents and brothers – but I never saw it in terms of life and death, or as unconditional. I had no idea that love could be sacrificial and never-ending, so you can imagine my complete surprise to find out that God's love for me went so far as Him sending His son to die for my sins. That's a difficult concept for anyone to wrap his mind around, but it was particularly overwhelming for me because I hated myself so much for being the special kid.

But the message I heard at camp was loud and clear and constant: *God demonstrated His love in that while we were still sinning, Christ died for us.*

"Love." Now there's a word that I believe has lost its true meaning. Our society has done a really good job of confusing us about what love is.

True story: When I was in the seventh grade, my music teacher decided to show our class the movie The West Side Story. There is a scene in that movie when Maria and Tony see each other for the first time at the school dance. The moment their eyes meet, the room and all the people in it become fuzzy and fade to black until it's just Tony and Maria in the room. They have eyes for no one but each other. They are suddenly and irrevocably in love.

Even after a few years had passed since I had watched that movie, I believed that that was how people fell in love. As a result of my faulty assumption, I left more than a few school dances disappointed at not having found my Maria.

When I was in high school, I watched entirely too much TV. There were all kinds of shows that molded my understanding of love and life in general. One such show, Melrose Place, messed me up for years. I could barely keep up with the ever-changing couplings of the residents of Melrose Place. The characters would date for an episode, have sex, and then in the next episode they would fall out of love and fall in love with someone else. Then a few more episodes down the road, they would figure out that no, they were still in love with that other person they had fallen out of love with, and the relational musical chairs game would start all over again. It seemed that love was all about the thrill of the chase, how attracted you were to someone, and how good the sex was.

The other thing about Melrose Place that I noticed is that everyone was beautiful and well-dressed. Even the garbage man was good looking, so I began believing that only beautiful people ever got a chance to experience the hot, passionate love that Hollywood is so skillful at portraying. And where did that leave me? Well, not in the best of spots, that's for sure!

At camp, I learned a word I had never heard before – agape – meaning unconditional love. It was a completely novel concept to me. A love that cannot be earned, or be paid for, and is freely given. Non-sexual and completely selfless. Who'd ever heard of such a thing? All you can do is receive it, be grateful and in turn show it to other people to the best of your abilities.

It took me all week long to grasp that there was nothing I could do to earn God's love, because He already loved me. His love was already there for the taking. All I needed to do was set aside my pride and come to a place where I was humble enough to do what little kids have no trouble doing: receive it and jump for joy, giving thanks.

Thursday night, my last at the camp, the speaker gave his final message. At the end of his message, he gave us the opportunity to receive the gift of eternal life by humbling ourselves before God and asking Jesus to be the king of our lives. That night, in a rustic chapel in Indiana, seven years after I was labeled special and began building my brick wall, I encountered the King of Kings, and I was anxious for his gift of salvation. I will never forget that day because it was the day that Jesus made me a new man, a saved man.

Once I realized that there was more to life than the wrapping paper, that God had a gift inside just for me, a gift that would provide me with the true meaning of love, my life has never been the same.

As I watched my daughter dive into another Christmas present, I wondered if God's heart melts the way mine did as I watched her for the first time understand the true meaning of the word "gift."

cartoon copyrighted by Mark Parisi, printed with permission

Chapter 10

Growing up, I didn't read very many books, but I loved the books I did read. I was a big fan of The Hardy Boys, though my attention span would only allow me to last about half the book. I still don't know what happened in about five books.

One book I did finish and love was "The Indian in the Cupboard." What boy wouldn't love a book about cowboys and Indians?

At the top of the list of all the books I enjoyed the most though were the "Choose Your Own Adventure" books. I loved the idea of having to flip forward 40 pages to find out what came next. For Special Ed students like myself, seeing more pages on the left side of the book is always a big boost to the morale, and is motivating.

As we dive into your story, I realize that each of you may be at a different place in your journey, so you need to, in essence, "choose your own adventure." That's why I've given you three choices to lead you into the next part of your adventure in reading this book. Read each of the following options first before making your choice.

Option I

As you have been reading this book, you have had questions about this so-called encounter with Christ. You have not yet had your own encounter, but would like to explore the idea a bit more. If you have never had an encounter with Christ and would like to know more, turn to page 137.

Option II

You have been reading for some time and you need a little break in the action. You are not ready to put the book down because you want to see what comes next, but in order to hang in there you need a little fun before you move any further. For a fun, quick break, turn to page 113.

Option III

You have been enjoying the book and the direction it has been leading you. You have been thinking about your own story and how much God has done in your life. You are not ready for the story to end and you desire to keep the good times rolling. To continue the journey that will lead to a hands-on project enabling you to record your greatest story, turn to page 117.

Interview with Bigfoot

Q: *How have Sasquatch been able to say hid-den for so long?*

A: Well I'm not sure if you can say we've done that good of a job at staying hidden. If we had, there wouldn't be so many people out there looking for us. Last I heard, there were some 3,000 or more sightings of my family over the years. Probably the biggest blow to the Sasquatch com-munity was back in 1967 when my Uncle Earl got filmed heading over to our place for dinner one night. We were doing so well keeping to ourselves, and then Uncle Earl had to go and blow it for us.

Fact: *On October 20, 1967, in northern Califor-nia, Roger Patterson and Robert Gimlin filmed what was thought to be a real life Sasquatch. Critics say the Patterson-Gimlin footage was faked, but every attempt to prove it was a hoax, or recreate it, has been unsuccessful.*

Chapter 11¹⁄₂

Fun Time Origami

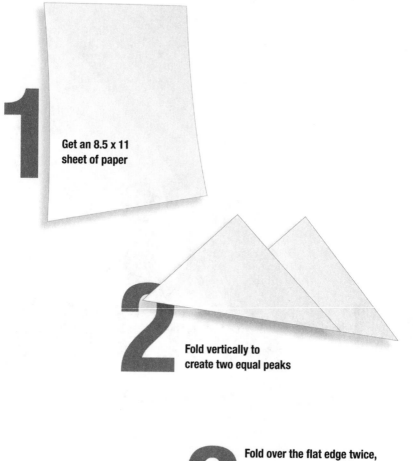

1 Get an 8.5 x 11 sheet of paper

2 Fold vertically to create two equal peaks

3 Fold over the flat edge twice, making the fold about .5 inch wide

4

Make a tube out of the paper, bringing together the two ends.
Make sure the rolled over edge is on the outside of the tube.
Tape the ends together, so that the paper looks like a little crown.

5

Fly the plane:

Place your first and second fingers, like they are
scissors between the two peaks of the crown.
Now throw (like you would throw a tennis ball or a baseball.
Watch it fly!

cartoon copyrighted by Mark Parisi, printed with permission

Chapter 12

Two-and-a-half years into a college degree, my speaking schedule was beginning to expand past weekends, and was starting to interfere with my classes. It was time to make a decision. I didn't know what to do. On the one hand, I was caught up in the idea that I needed a college degree in order to have a good job, but on the other, I felt that God was asking me to take a leap of faith and to commit myself to a more vigorous pursuit of ministry. I met with my student advisor to seek his counsel. I was torn and afraid of what would happen if I made the wrong choice. Thankfully, my advisor had some good wisdom for me, "This college is not going anywhere, and you can always return, but if God is opening a door for you, you should not pass that up."

At the time, most of my events were taking place in central Indiana, so after I said goodbye to the dorms of Anderson University, I moved in with a friend who kindly offered to put me up while things got rolling with my speaking. Things weren't as simple as I had hoped they would be. I learned very quickly that calling up local churches and telling them that I could draw with chalk didn't open up doors. Ironically, this was turning out to be the one job where having connections with "The Boss," wasn't going to help!

Yet, there were bills to pay and I had to get a regular job so I could pay for food, gas and art supplies. The only job that made sense was being a waiter. It was flexible, paid pretty well, and I'd done it before, so I knew what I was getting into.

For those of you who have not had the pleasure of waiting on tables, let me just say – it's no easy job. It is so much more than just bringing people food and refilling drinks. Let me put it to you this way: I have had a chance to speak in front of 70,000 people in the Pontiac Silver Dome, before they blew it up, and I don't know what was more stressful, standing before that many people or waiting on tables. Having five tables of hungry people is no walk in the park. Work a whiny child into that mix, and things can get downright ugly!

I got a job at the Olive Garden. Getting back into the routine of being a server was hard, but after a month, I was Mr. Olive Garden! I could handle five tables at a time without letting anyone's drinks dry out or the breadbaskets get empty. A few months into the job, I was making enough to pay the bills and buy chalk and paper. I spoke an average of four times a month, wondering if things would ever pick up and if I'd be stuck being a waiter for the rest of my life. Unbeknownst to me, working in the food service industry was not that good for me.

Here's why: While customers are enjoying the wonderful ambiance of their quaint booths, back in the kitchen it is pure pandemonium. During the lunch or dinner rush, when the restaurant is filled with hungry customers, their kind and polite waiters will frequently transform werewolf-like into angry, annoyed, and often vulgar people as soon as they enter the kitchen. Being a server is a high-pressure job, and as any server will tell you, it is much better to blow off steam in the kitchen than in front of your customers.

Every night I waited on tables was like being part of an R-rated movie. The censor had left the building! I really expanded my vocabulary those few months; unfortunately most of the words I learned were not fit for polite conversation. The first few weeks at the restaurant, I could hardly believe the way some people talked. Every time someone swore, it was like nails on the chalkboard for me. Soon, though, I found that I could just ignore the cussing. I stopped hearing it.

Then one Friday night, after things hit crazy mode, I began to experience the effects of being in a worldly environment. I got quadruple sat, which in plain English means that I got four tables within minutes of each other (and that's BAD!). My customers were obviously all very hungry; I thought I saw one guy eating the sugar packets. Nonetheless, everything was going okay. All tables had their drinks, bread had been distributed, orders put in, the tables were all at various stages of salad consumption, and all I had to do now was bring out the dinners.

One small glitch: I had forgotten to place the sugar packet eater's order for lasagna. This is never a good thing, but on a busy night, it could only spell disaster. I went to explain and apologize, but the guy was not having it. He wanted his food NOW; only my head on a platter would make a suitable substitution. I had to do some significant sucking up, bringing him and his date complimentary drinks. Where was that lasagna?!

I ran into the kitchen for what seemed like the 100th time in the last 10 minutes, and there it was! Thank God! I quickly put the lasagna on a tray and hit the salad bar to load up a bowl for another guest. I turned away from my precious lasagna for a moment, a moment I tell you, and when I turned back to grab the tray, to my horror, the lasagna was gone! I quickly scanned the area hoping to spot the culprit who had taken my food, but no luck. Right at that moment, I finally gained a complete understanding of what my mom meant when she'd said through clenched teeth, "I've had it up to here with you kids!!" bringing her hand up to her temple, palm down, and giving us a stare that could make a grown man cry. Before I could even give it any thought, I opened my mouth and yelled over the din of the kitchen, "Who the F-Bomb, took my F-Bomb lasagna?!?"

A few of the other servers just laughed at me and one of them even walked by and said, "Now you're a true server. Welcome to the family."

Just then, a fresh plate of lasagna appeared in the kitchen window. One of the other waiters grabbed it, put it on my tray, and said, "Here you go! This sure looks like your F-Bomb lasagna."

We all laughed as if nothing happened. I walked out of the kitchen feeling a little cool, like I had just been initiated into a new club. I hadn't really connected with most of the servers until then, but now it suddenly felt like maybe I could hang out with them and have a good time.

When I got back to the kitchen, I was greeted by a few more F-Bombs from my coworkers, who now saw me as one of their own. Without a second thought, I spewed out a few colorful words in response to their comments. I began to carry on with my work duties, not thinking much about what had happened or the line that I had crossed. Thankfully, God was looking out for me even when I wasn't.

Who knows where my lack of conviction and discipline would have taken me. Sin loves to thrive insidiously in our lives. A little compromise here, a bit over there. Oh, what's the harm, I'm not hurting anyone. And slowly, bit by bit, white lie by white lie, we grow further and further away from God and from who Christ wants us to be.

But God had sent me Carl.

When I started working at Olive Garden, I remember thinking as I met Carl, he's a bit old to be a waiter. I was surprised he wasn't a manager, but was in the trenches with the rest of us college-aged kids. I liked Carl from the get-go. He was a quiet guy and kept mostly to himself, but he had an air of serenity about him that set him apart from everyone else and made it nice to have him around. One night, a few shifts into my server tour of duty, Carl was put in charge of teaching me the joys of rolling silverware into paper napkins. We talked as we worked, and I learned that Carl's last few months had been rough. He and his family were living out in Colorado when suddenly his wife left him for another guy. She then proceeded to take the kids and move to Indianapolis. Carl quit a prestigious job and followed his kids to Indy because he couldn't bear to be separated from them. So now, he was working at Olive Garden until a job opened up in his field of expertise. I remember listening to his story thinking, how horrible. But Carl was okay with it. He shared how God had been teaching him so much, and that his relationship with his kids was better than ever now that he didn't have a big corporate job that kept him at the office 70 hours a week. Carl wore a small pin in the shape of a cross on his collar and he made it pretty clear that God was in charge of his life. In turn, I shared my struggles, hopes and dreams about becoming a full-time speaker and evangelist. As we got to the end of the tedious task, Carl gave me some encouragement and told me that he'd pray for me. That was the most we ever spoke.

Back in the kitchen, following my little F-Bomb moment, it was just Carl and I. Carl looked over at me and said something that forever pierced my heart, "Ben, you know something? We have to live in this world, but we are not of this world. Remember who you are." And suddenly I realized how far I had slipped.

It was quite ironic that I had started my job at Olive Garden so that I could pay my bills to stay in Indianapolis and begin working in full-time ministry. I wanted to get up in front of people and tell people about Jesus Christ and yet, somehow, in the months that I worked at Olive Garden, I shared my faith there once. ONCE! With Carl.

I knew then that at Olive Garden, the world was impacting me more than I was impacting it. I needed to regroup and refocus. That night, I put in my notice. It was the last time I would ever serve lasagna.

* * * * * * * *

Why hadn't I told anyone but Carl about who I really was? Why didn't I share about the things that were important to me with my coworkers? To be honest, I don't really remember. It may have been that I was embarrassed or insecure about what people would think of me. I had spent so long trying to fit in as a kid, that even as a young adult, I was still driven by that impulse for acceptance. Or maybe, I just didn't think that anyone would be interested. My co-workers were so far removed from who I knew to be "regular" church-goers that on some level, I thought that it would have been pointless to say anything anyway. Another thought I have is that I may not have known where to start or how to open the conversation. It's not like I could walk into the kitchen and say, "Hey, everyone, so I was reading my Bible the other day and it says that we all need to pick up our crosses and follow Jesus. How about it?"

In retrospect, I just didn't have enough confidence in my story and the story of Christ. Did you know that it wasn't until I had been speaking full-time for three years that I actually started sharing my story about growing up with learning disabilities and going to the FCA camp and meeting Bill Leach there? Hard to believe, but true!

When I first started getting up on stage and sharing the Gospel, I was not what you would call a confident speaker. I'd share a story from the Bible, talk about what it meant to me, and then draw – that was about it. Back then, the drawings would take me a lot longer to finish than they do now, so I didn't have to speak very much; I just let the drawing and the lightshow do most of that.

After I got married and moved to Chicago, my wife and I started attending Christ Church of Oak Brook where we volunteered to work with the high school students. One day, the youth pastor asked me to share my testimony with the group. I was a little taken aback, but agreed to do it. It was strange being up front going into such detail about myself and what God had been doing with my life, but I saw that the students were all captivated by the story. Normally a rowdy group, they gave me their full attention. Afterwards, I got great feedback from many of them, and at the end of the night, my wife pulled me aside and said, "You really need to be sharing THAT with all your groups. That is a powerful story!" And suddenly, my favorite verse – Jeremiah 29:11 – took on a whole new meaning!

You may be thinking, Yeah, Ben Glenn, but your story is pretty cool. If I had a story like yours, I'd share it too. My story is nowhere near as interesting.

The truth is that my story started getting interesting when I crossed paths with Jesus. He is the one responsible for all my adventures – well, at least the good ones! I'm sure your story is as interesting as mine, just different, that's all.

We all have a story. Just like Levi, just like me, just like you, we all have a story of how Jesus touched our lives. Each story is touching to ourselves, and each story will touch others if we will reach out with it, and share it. Just like the story of Bigfoot, it will live and breathe once we get it out there.

In case you're having a hard time recalling all the moments in your life that will give you a story you feel good about sharing, at the end of this book, I'm going to ask you all kinds of questions. When you're done answering, you will have a fine start to your story. Don't forget, too, that your story will continue growing and expanding as you keep walking with Christ.

So when you close the back cover of this book, I want you to remember just one thing: simply tell your story! When you're sitting on a plane and someone strikes up a conversation, tell your story. When you hang out at lunch with your friends, tell your story. When you're eating dinner with your family, tell your story. When you're in the locker room after a football or basketball or volleyball game, share your story. It does not matter how you tell your story, it does not matter where you tell your story, it does not matter when you tell your story, it only matters that do tell your story.

Why? Because your story will have ripple effects that you are not even aware of, for both yourself, and the world you live in.

Interview with Bigfoot

Q: What does the Sasquatch community have planned for the future?

A: Well there's a bunch of us that would like to come out of the woods finally, like my brother Chewbacca. However, the old timers are having too much fun messing around with all the Bigfoot chasers. I personally am hoping to take my talents to Hollywood, maybe do a sequel to Harry and the Hendersons, or something. Either way, we Sasquatch are here to stay.

Fact: *Bigfoot is Big Business. While working on this book and trying to find some fun things to add to the book, I discovered Bigfoot is big! There are tons of websites, associations, movies, books, t-shirts and even coffee cups that all have to do with finding and believing in the Sasquatch. If you want to have some fun, Google Bigfoot and enjoy the ride.*

Remembering Your Story

Finally you've come to the part of the book where you get to focus on your own story and why it's important to tell it. I'm going to ask you a bunch of really personal questions and I want you to think really hard and answer as honestly as you can. No, you do not need to email me your answers and there is no right or wrong way to answer each one, but you should go get a notebook and some writing instruments right now! If you're having a hard time finding something to write on, I've got you covered as there are some lined pages at the end of this book ready for you to scribble your thoughts. Okay! Are you ready? Here we go:

I shared with you about the anger I felt after being labeled in chapter 3. Have you ever had a time when you felt such anger? What happened to create such anger inside of you?

We can do a lot with anger. Some people bottle their anger up until one day the bottle breaks. Some lash out at others. Some people like me become beasts on the football field. What did you, or what do you do with your anger? How do you feel in those moments after you let out your anger? Have you ever been angry with God like Levi? Why?

Are you still angry at God?

If you are still angry at God, read John 3:16, Romans 5:8 and Jeremiah 29:11. How do you feel now? Do you think God has a plan for your life? What do you think that plan might look like? (Compare what you're angry about to what God tells us in these two passages.)

Have you ever felt all alone in life? When did this happen and why?

Did you share this feeling with anyone around you? Did you share this feeling with God? If not, then why not?

If so, how did it make you feel?

What are some thoughts that come to your mind when you hear that Jesus loves you?

Do you think you're a hard person to love?

If so, describe the things in you that you think are hard to love?

If Jesus were sitting next to you right now, what are some of the things He may say about you? Why do you think He feels this way about you?

When was the first time you heard the story of Jesus? What did you think of it?

Was it easy to believe that Jesus died on the cross for you or did it take a while for you to accept this? If it took some time, what was the thing that convinced you the Cross was for you?

Where were you when you gave your life to Jesus?

What was life like right before you received the gift of Salvation?

After you gave your life to God, did you tell your family and/ or friends? How did they respond? How did their response make you feel?

If you haven't shared your story with your family or friends, what do you think some of the reasons may be for keeping you from telling them what God has done in your life?

If your family has a relationship with Jesus, how do you feel your coming to know Jesus changed things at home?

If your family does not know Jesus, how do you feel your coming to know Jesus has changed things at home?

How has giving your life to Jesus changed your life?

How do see your relationship with Jesus? Is he a good friend, a distant relative, a father figure, a boss you're afraid of? What kind of a relationship do you think Jesus would like to have with you?

In the same way I struggled at the Olive Garden with my faith, have you ever blown it? In what ways have you compromised in your walk with Jesus? How do you get back on track?

Have you ever been in a situation where you were with someone and there was something inside of you prompting you to share your story? Is so, did you share your story, and what was the response of the person you shared it with?

Have you ever had that prompting and missed your chance to share? How did that make you feel? What do you think it was prompting you to share? What do you think it was that kept you from listening to the prompting in your heart?

I am 6 foot 4 and I am scared to death of spiders. I am also sometimes afraid of what people think. If I was hanging out with you and I shared with you my fear of what people thought of me or my fear of telling people my story, what would you say to help me overcome my fears?

If we were hanging out around a camp fire roasting marshmallows and I asked you to tell me your story, how would you start? (Once upon a time does not count!)

Okay, so hopefully all these questions have jogged your memory about where, how and why your walk with Jesus started and what has happened since then.

cartoon copyrighted by Mark Parisi, printed with permission

Simply Salvation

What would you say if I told you it was simple? You would most likely say that I was nuts. But it is simple, and I believe that is the way that Christ intended it to be. Too many times our vision of true Christianity is obscured by human agendas, denominational disputes, and the media. We are unable to fully understand God's offer of salvation and His message of hope.

The two stories you just read are stories about two people in need of one thing, a message of hope. It is sad that sometimes it takes a dire situation to allow a person to understand the true message of the cross. I assure you that neither the leper nor I were thinking about what the media thought about God when we were in our lowest of lows. We were thinking one thing: HELP!

Let's say for a moment, that we are able to set aside all the controversy about Christianity that riles people up and creates prejudices and differences. Now let's look closely at who Jesus was and why He died.

In the New Testament, Romans 3:23 tells us "For all have sinned and fallen short of the glory of God." There is nothing we can do or say that will ever change the fact that you and I are not "basically good" as some folks like to believe. Look around and see what "man" is capable of. I don't know about you, but I have a hard time believing that given the choice, people will generally do the right thing. Even when we want to do the right thing, a lot of times we can't or won't and that's the power of sin.

Despite this, God still loves us and wants to be with us. Unfortunately, our sin and God's holiness cannot mix. Why? It's cosmically impossible. The laws of the universe that God set in motion do not permit this. In the same way that it cannot be day and night at the same time, a sinner cannot come into God's presence.

But God came up with the solution to this huge dilemma. A sacrifice would be required. A sacrifice would bring balance and harmony. The death of an innocent as a payment for all the terrible sins committed by humankind would be needed. Who was perfect and pure enough to offer the counterweight to such a terrible burden of sin? No one other than God's own son – Jesus.

If it's impossible to wrap your mind around this entire concept, just keep this in mind: Your sins separate you from God, but the death of Jesus, as a sacrifice for your life, has taken that sin, wiped it clean, and made it possible for you to be with God for all eternity. The catch? You need to believe and to accept the gift of Christ's sacrifice for your very own.

Some will say that it all sounds like a far-fetched fairytale. That's true if you try to figure it out using human wisdom. It will never make sense. It's all about faith, child-like faith at that. Reach down beyond your intellect, into your very gut, your soul and see if there is a God-shaped hole in there somewhere. If you're really honest with yourself, you will acknowledge that there are times when you feel that something is missing in your life. This world likes to make us believe that what we're missing is more food, or sex, or money, or new clothes, or better parents, or a something else, as long as it's not God. But it is God.

If you've read this far, I believe that God has been knocking on the door of your heart. If you've been searching for love in "all the wrong places," I'm happy to tell you that you are now right where you need to be.

Earlier, I shared one of my favorite verses with you: "For I know the plans I have for you, declares the Lord, plans to prosper you and not to harm you, plans to give you hope and a future." It continues in verse 13, "You will seek me and find me when you seek me with all your heart. I will be found by you," declares the Lord (Jeremiah 29:11). The Message, a version of the Bible re-worded to sound more like the way we speak in this day and age, says it like this: "I know what I'm doing. I have it all planned out – plans to take care of you, not abandon you, plans to give you a future you hope for. When you call on me, when you come and pray to me, I'll listen. When you come looking for me, you'll find me. Yes, when you get serious about finding me and want it more than anything else, I'll make sure you won't be disappointed."

I'm sure you've heard the saying "Seek and you shall find." It's also a verse out of the Bible. What have you been seeking lately?

Whatever you may have thought about God up until this point, consider this: God loves you. John 3:16 says, "For God so loved the world that he gave his one and only Son, that whoever believes in him shall not perish but have eternal life. For God did not send his Son into the world to condemn the world, but to save the world through him."

Once again, it is time for you to choose your own adventure. Where your story leads next is up to you.

Option one. You're still not sure about God and his plans. You like the way your story is going and having a relationship with God or receiving the gift of Salvation is not a priority right now. If Option One is where you are right now, then you've reached the end of the book. Thanks for reading! I hope that at the very least I've given you something to think about. If you continue seeking the truth, you will find it. God bless you!

Option two. You know God loves you and sent his Son to die for you and you choose to accept Gods gift of salvation. If option two is your choice then keep on reading.

God made becoming a part of his family quite simple. There is no big test to take or obstacle course to go through. Like it says in Romans 10:9, all you have to do is believe and ask God to forgive your sins and God will welcome you with open arms. You can make up your own prayer, but here is one that I usually use when I pray with folks who want to make that first-time commitment:

Dear God,
I know that I'm a sinner and I am sorry for living a life that does not honor you. I believe that Jesus is your perfect Son who died on the cross for me. I thank you for the free gift of Salvation that you offer me and I believe by faith that Jesus is my Savior. Thank you for my new identity in you as a child of God. Give me the courage to seek you more than I seek this world. Help mold my life and help me to become the person you always intended me to be. In Jesus' Name, I pray these things.
Amen.

*After you spend some time
with God, feel free to jump back to
page 117 and continue reading.*

About the author...

When he was in the third grade, Ben was diagnosed with a Learning Disability associated with his reading and writing skills. Had the definition of ADHD existed back then, he would have been diagnosed with that as well. Like most LD/ADHD challenged students, Ben spent the greater majority of his school career struggling to keep up, wondering what was wrong with him, having little guidance and support, going through highs and lows and dealing with self-esteem issues.

Fortunately, Ben didn't allow his challenges to get in the way of becoming a success story. Through trial and error, significant life events, and special people, Ben has learned how to tap into the talents and positive traits that come along with having a Learning Disability & ADHD.

A full-time speaker and entertainer since 1994, Ben has traveled all over the world to share his inspiring, dynamic and creative presentations with people of all ages and backgrounds.

Finally, as much as Ben loves being a speaker and performing artist, he loves being a husband and father more. Married for over eleven years, he, his wife and two daughters live in a great little city called Indianapolis.

Footnotes

Footnotes

Footnotes

_____

_____

_____

_____

_____

_____

_____

_____

_____

_____

_____

_____

Footnotes

Footnotes

Footnotes

Footnotes

Footnotes

Footnotes

Footnotes

Footnotes

Footnotes

Footnotes

Footnotes

Footnotes